Differences

Differences

Topographies of Contemporary Architecture

Ignasi de Solà-Morales translated by Graham Thompson

edited by Sarah Whiting

This book was set in Janson by The MIT Press and was printed and bound in the United States of America.

Library of Congress Cataloging-in-Publication Data

Solà-Morales Rubió, Ignasi, 1942–
    [Diferencias. English]
    Differences : topographies of contemporary architecture / Ignasi de Solà-Morales ; translated by Graham Thompson ; edited by Sarah Whiting.
        p.   cm. — (Writing architecture)
    Includes bibliographical references and index.
    ISBN 0-262-69190-6 (pbk. : alk. paper)
    1. Architecture, Modern—20th century—Themes, motives. 2. Architecture and philosophy.   I. Whiting, Sarah.   II. Title. III. Series.
NA680.S6413   1997
724′.6—dc20   96-34298
                                                                CIP

For Lali

Subjectifying the Modern

In Deleuze, as in the phenome-
nological tradition, one finds the
reading or description of reality as
something that must be built,
designed, as a process from the sub-
ject, as work to be done, drafted . . .

—Ignasi de Solà-Morales

Ignasi de Solà-Morales would be
the first to admit that pairing the
seemingly opposing influences of
contemporary French theory, particularly the work of Gilles Deleuze, and
the philosophical tradition of phenomenology, particularly as articulated by
Edmund Husserl and Martin Heidegger,
is unorthodox. Joining these philosophical
inheritances, however, allows de Solà-
Morales to reposition the human subject without referencing a specifically classical humanist

subject or obliging a renunciation of the object. Contrary to the canonical tenet that modernism successfully suppressed the subject in favor of a democratizing, equalizing objectivity, de Solà-Morales demonstrates that the subject plays an integral role in modernism's very definition, and accordingly suggests that that subject—unjustly slain by such claims to modernist objectivity and poststructuralist nihilism—should be resurrected.

The dual influences of phenomenology and Deleuze provoke de Solà-Morales to design, draft, and ultimately build an evocative account of modernism's lineage of subjectivity that reaches both back beyond phenomenology and forward beyond poststructuralism, ultimately culminating in a provocative presentation of our contemporary multitude of fluid topographies. Reflecting his dual career as architect and theorist, de Solà-Morales's writing becomes a project: his texts can be understood as a *critical formalism*, a form of writing that both calls existing forms of aesthetic criticism into question and also criticizes aesthetic form.

Simplified textbook formulae frequently assert that by the 1920s and 1930s, the International Style, CIAM, *Neue Sachlichkeit*, constructivism, *De Stijl*, Fordism, and Taylorism had rendered modernism virtually synonymous with objectivity. Functional objectivity and economic pragmatism, these abecedarian narratives propose, successfully dislodged Beaux-Arts classicism's humanist aesthetics, remaining essentially unchallenged until the 1960s when a social agenda, as articulated by Team X, replaced the functional one articulated by CIAM. Postmodernism's return to a classical aesthetic, such accounts conclude, was modern objectivity's ultimate death knell, and simultaneously served as the clarion call for a humanist return to the subject.

But the subject's challenge to objectivity had actually been initiated already from within modernism. If prewar high modernism can be encapsulated by Hannes Meyer's pithy 1928 definition of building, "All things in this world are a product of the formula: (function times economy),"[1] then already by 1930 Mies van der Rohe warned of the dangers of such extreme objectivism : "Whether we build high or low, with steel and glass, tells us nothing about the value of the building. . . . For the meaning and right of every age, including our own, consists solely in providing the spirit with the necessary prerequisites for its existence."[2] And by 1947 Frederick Kiesler articulated a modernist return to the subject, proclaiming, "I oppose to the mysticism of Hygiene, which is the superstition of 'Functional Architecture', the realities of a Magical Architecture rooted in the totality of the human being, and not in the blessed or accursed parts of this being."[3] Although this shift away from functional objectivity appears sudden, it is not hard to understand how World War II's horrific war-machine functionalism might compel such a swift turn to a more sympathetic, accessible architecture, focusing more on sensory than on economic impacts of formal manipulation.

Although postwar formalist production responded directly to its political context, it also responded to a prewar aesthetic lineage of subjectivity and ethics. If one dates modernism as beginning not in the 1920s but with Immanuel Kant's *Critique of Judgment* of 1790, then a provocative subjective thread begins to appear, surreptitiously weaving through even the most seemingly objective modernist moments. For Kant, experience was integral to our knowledge of objects in the world around us—they could not be described in purely objective, nonexperiential terms. The danger that such a system of subjective aestheticism could lead to indulgent individualism is avoided by recourse to a higher moral order or law. Accordingly, the Kantian subject forever moves between the phenomenal order of instinct and desire and the noumenal order of moral imperatives.

Kant's definition of aesthetic judgment influenced the developing discipline of aesthetics, whose early protagonists sought to transform his theory into a cognitive science, combining psychology and physiology. In 1870, Robert Vischer, then a graduate student in philosophy, wrote a dissertation that analyzed the subjective element of aesthetic contemplation. Among the many neologisms Vischer coined in this work was *empathy*, or emotional projection, a term that presaged Edmund Husserl's philosophy of phenomenology. For Vischer, an aesthetic object engaged the viewer's emotions, and that engagement was as integral to the work as its form: "in the visual arts," he wrote, "it is not a question of content or form but of the power of its image, of its phenomenality."[4] The research of aesthetic formalism that developed in the late nineteenth and early twentieth centuries, led by Adolf von Hildebrand, Conrad Fiedler, Heinrich Wölfflin, August Schmarsow, and others, furthered Vischer's investigation into the relationship between the subject and the object, focusing first on issues of visual perception and ultimately translating the relationship into fully sensorial, experiential terms.

This turn-of-the-century investigation of the relation between the subject and the object, coupled with the political and social climate of the 1930s and 1940s, influenced the development of phenomenology. If one can generalize that the aesthetic formalists tried to systematize the sensations, one could add that Edmund Husserl's philosophy of phenomenology, contrariwise, tried to sensationalize the system. Although Husserl began the project of phenomenology at the turn of the century, the tenor of his writing changed toward the end of his life as the specter of fascism began to manifest itself in his native Germany. Recalling

Mies's 1930 call for a value or spirituality to be restored to building, Husserl's final texts, particularly his *Crisis of European Sciences and Transcendental Phenomenology* of 1936, described an urgent need to subordinate scientific rationalism to the admittedly more vulnerable realm of subjective perception. He advocated developing a "universal science of subjectivity," where individual life would be balanced by a notion of the *Lebenswelt* or "life-world," rather than subordinated to the rational world of science. Recalling the Kantian subject's suspension between the phenomenal and noumenal realms, Husserl's notion of the *Lebenswelt* implies a universal sense of moral order that overlaps with, but does not exclude, subjective individualism. Husserl sensed that the political and social crisis of his day threatened this balance by replacing the *Lebenswelt* order with a totalitarian one. Concern for its restoration impelled the philosopher to propose that "we can attend to it [the *Lebenswelt*] in its generality and, with sufficient care, fix it once and for all in a way equally accessible to all."[5]

Husserl's implication that the crisis could be resolved, and that such an action would benefit *all*, introduces the concept of *social* subjectivity. Although Kant's theory of morals acknowledged the social—his maxim of action states that one should act as if one's action were to be translated into a maxim for all—Husserl's call for action implies a certain agency for determining actual social life, rather than acting under the influence of an assumed order. The climate of crisis instilled a sense of urgency, suggesting the necessity for the modernist subject to take an active rather than passive role in defining a new social order. Such calls to action also occurred within architecture. In their short manifesto "Nine Points on Monumentality" of 1943, Sigfried Giedion, Josep Lluís Sert, and Fernand Léger declared that architects had a responsibility to articulate the terms of postwar democratic society, claiming that politicians could only imagine a society organized along nineteenth-century lines; only the architect, planner, or artist could envision the future.[6] This trio of expatriates never articulated their idea of a democratic society in terms other than abstract visions of an ethically cohesive, societal *mass*, however. The good intentions underlying their—and others'—efforts to counter the postwar societal crisis never produced either a new subject or a new society; ultimately, their abstract visions only reinforced a normative, conservative societal conformism that has itself been under attack since the radical critique of the 1960s.

This failure poses a dilemma for de Solà-Morales, who, unlike many critics writing today, is not willing to jettison the entire foundation of this postwar desire to restore a certain ethical order to the world. Nevertheless, he recognizes the utopianism and reductivism underlying many of these efforts, and is unable to tolerate their lack of diversity and individuality. He favors a humanism, but a nonconforming humanism that acknowledges the 1960s critique.

Gilles Deleuze, de Solà-Morales's second strain of influence, provides the theoretical means by which this theoretical impasse can be breached. He, along with his collaborator, Félix Guattari, provides a flexible model for the contemporary subject, but one that does not entirely abandon a notion of ethical, societal life in favor of wanton, selfish individuality. As Michel Foucault writes in his preface to their *Anti-Oedipus: Capitalism and Schizophrenia*, "One might say that *Anti-Oedipus* is an *Introduction to Non-Fascist Life*." Foucault elaborates this description with a Deleuze-derived imperative: "Do not demand of politics that it restore the 'rights' of the individual, as philosophy has defined them. The individual is the product of power. What is needed is to 'de-individualize' by means of multiplication and displacement, diverse combinations. The group must not be the organic bond uniting hierarchized individuals, but a constant generator of de-individualization."[7] Deleuze and Guattari articulate a model that allows for a certain independent subjectivity, but within the context of a world that still affects the subject in predictable as well as spontaneous ways: a model that allows for a mutual and ever-changing interaction between subject and object.

Armed with Deleuze's delirious models of social multiplicity, de Solà-Morales retreads the ground of the 1940s and 1950s, the period of phenomenology's greatest influence. In addressing topics as varied as Mies van der Rohe's parallels with artistic minimalism, the discipline of architectural criticism, and the rhetoric that constructs complex relationships between architecture and engineering, de Solà-Morales repeatedly returns to the key themes of individuality, space, and place. Like Max Horkheimer and Theodor Adorno, de Solà-Morales believes that "the task to be accomplished is not the conservation of the past, but the redemption of hopes of the past,"[8] the redemption of optimism in the face of contemporary pessimism. In constructing his analyses of past and present practice, de Solà-Morales succeeds in establishing a critical collaboration with practice, without succumbing to the two traps of nostalgia (critical collusion) or nihilism (radical critique). His texts, which try to define moments of intensity where architectural, artistic, societal, cultural, historical, ethical, and political forces intersect, are intended to provoke the reader, not by the methods of formalist estrangement, whereby the viewer is shocked into looking carefully at something familiar—rendered unfamiliar, *unstable*, by its changed context—but by another form of shock in which the reader recognizes the potential gathered in an instant of *stability* formed by the intersection of multiple moments of high intensity. Such instants can be illustrated, in conclusion, with an image elaborated in another book of Deleuze and Guattari, *What Is Philosophy?*:

In a violently poetic text, [D. H.] Lawrence describes what produces poetry: people are constantly putting up an umbrella that shelters them and on the underside of which they draw a firmament and write their conventions and opinions. But poets, artists, make a slit in the umbrella, they tear open the firmament itself, to let in a bit of free and windy chaos and to frame in a sudden light a vision that appears through the rent—Wordsworth's spring or Cézanne's apple, the silhouettes of Macbeth or Ahab. . . . Art indeed struggles with chaos, but it does so in order to bring forth a vision that illuminates it for an instant, a Sensation. . . . Art is not chaos but a composition of chaos that yields the vision or sensation, so that it constitutes, as Joyce says, a *chaosmos*, a composed chaos—neither foreseen nor preconceived.[9]

In his essays, Ignasi de Solà-Morales, perhaps more gently than violently, also tears open the firmament. These tears, or *events*, as he calls them, form Deleuzean moments of intensity, intersections of various lines—pasts, presents, and futures that coincide in a moment that reveals them all, revealing their contingencies as well as their effects. De Solà-Morales's desire to focus on these instantaneous moments of architectural intensity reveals an optimism that counters the atmosphere of cynicism and nihilism that has enveloped the culture of architecture ever since economic recession and political conservatism burst the bubble of postmodern positivism. His writing offers an optimistic but not utopian note with which to end the millennium.

Sarah Whiting

Notes

1. Hannes Meyer, "Building," in *Programs and Manifestoes on 20th-Century Architecture*, ed. Ulrich Conrads (Cambridge: MIT Press, 1984), 117.

2. Ludwig Mies van der Rohe, "The New Era," in ibid., 123.

3. Frederick Kiesler, "Magical Architecture," in ibid., 151.

4. Robert Vischer, as cited in the introduction to Harry Francis Mallgrave and Eleftherios Ikonomou, *Empathy, Form, and Space: Problems in German Aesthetics 1873–1893* (Santa Monica: Getty Center for the History of Art and the Humanities, 1994), 27.

5. Edmund Husserl, *The Crisis of European Sciences and Transcendental Phenomenology* (Evanston: Northwestern University Press, 1970), 139.

6. Sigfried Giedion, José Luis Sert, and Fernand Léger, "Nine Points on Monumentality," in *Architecture Culture 1943–1968*, ed. Joan Ockman and Edward Eigen (New York: Columbia Books of Architecture and Rizzoli, 1993), 29–30.

7. Michel Foucault, preface to Gilles Deleuze and Félix Guattari, *Anti-Oedipus: Capitalism and Schizophrenia* (Minneapolis: University of Minnesota Press, 1983), xiii–iv.

8. Max Horkheimer and Theodor Adorno, *Dialectic of Enlightenment*, trans. John Cumming (New York: Continuum, 1991), xv.

9. Gilles Deleuze and Félix Guattari, *What Is Philosophy?*, trans. Hugh Tomlinson and Graham Burchell (New York: Columbia University Press, 1994), 203–204.

Differences

This book seeks to be more than a mere collection of my published articles over the past few years. Of course it does assemble these texts, each one originally intended as a means of generating a larger discussion in response to a particular situation. The chapter titles bear witness to these various starting points, while the editorial note at the end indicates the specific publication or debate for which they were originally written. But a skein of recurring threads runs through all of the texts, in such a way that a number of ideas modulate through their several parts. Although it seems to me virtually impossible to construct a systematic discourse from these ideas, once assembled into a collection they have begun to construct their own conversation throughout these pages. The circularity of the themes, which I trust will present themselves to the reader over the course of this book, was the factor that persuaded me to bring together a selection of the texts I have written over the past eight years or more, reflecting as these do a way of thinking contemporary architecture. I find myself not only incapable but unwilling to compose a treatise or a compendium. In some sense, this book should be understood instead as a *flexible manifesto*, for it relies upon the modern tradition of the manifesto in its aim to provoke, but it does not subscribe to the totalizing singularity that often motivated these modernist proclamations.

One of the terms that most frequently appears in the course of the following chapters is *crisis*. I use the term with reference to historical situations where it is possible to perceive fractures dividing the consciousness that architecture, the arts, and culture have had of their own identity and the tasks specific to them. Circulating throughout my reflections here is the hypothesis that the history of the architecture of this century is marked by a series of critical episodes, some of which parallel crises in economics, politics, and society. Each of these crises marks a moment of change within the seemingly continuous tradition of the modernist project, and each, in a process analogous to that of nuclear fission, involves not only the disappearance of the previous material state but above all the release of new energies whose expansion will take place in new, and until that moment inconceivable, directions. As Ortega y Gasset wrote in his *Esquema de las Crisis*, every situation of this nature is a situation of extreme consciousness, hyperawareness, and also loneliness. The crisis, the crises, of this century's architecture are parallel to the crises of art, of culture, and thus of the collective consciousness.

Our terms *crisis* and *critique* are derived from the same common root in Greek and subsequently in Latin: κρίσις, *crisis*. In medicine, the crisis is the decisive moment that will lead to either health or death. In law, the crisis is the passing of judgment, the judge's decision that distinguishes between the legitimate and the illegitimate. The terms *judgment* and *decision* are thus inseparable from crisis and

also from criticism. Both are mediated by a third signification of the original Greek root, which is *separation*. The crisis is the time that separates the acute illness from its
resolution, for better or for worse. As constituted by the
judge's verdict, the crisis is the moment separating the trial
from the passing of the sentence.

To engage in the critique of architecture means situating oneself inside the crisis and embracing both hyperawareness and loneliness. The perception of crises
constitutes the starting point of criticism. Being conscious
of them means diagnosing them, expressing a judgment
that separates the different principles that come together
in a given historical situation. Architectural criticism is not
a literary genre, nor is it a profession. It is, above all, an intellectual attitude by means of which discourse becomes—in
loneliness and in consciousness of the crisis—judgment,
separation, and decision.

The description of all that is happening in the
panorama of present-day architecture might seem to be an
exercise of classification if we were convinced that architecture is a matter of genres, types, and species structurally
capable of sustaining such a classification. Such a hypothesis underlies a certain mode of criticism that presupposes
the existence of groups, tendencies, currents, or even styles,
permitting a morphological ordering of all there is to be
known about a given reality. *Gray* or *white*, *modern* or *classical*, *organicist* or *mechanist*, *apocalyptic* or *integrated*, and so
on, are the conceptual pairings that have replaced the old
system of stylistic classification that art history and architectural history imported from so-called natural history.

Yet when we acknowledge that what constitutes the
significant core of a given phenomenon is not so much its
belonging to a particular genre or type as its radical singularity, the problem becomes that of the instruments with

which we are to recognize that singularity. In recent years historiography has sought to address the delicate question of how to analyze the specific as the specific. This is, from the perspective of philosophy, the problem identified by phenomenology: that of arriving at knowledge of things in themselves on the basis of a science, grounded not in abstract principles but in representation. Rather than imposing a framework, or a categorizing system, *upon* something, phenomenology seeks to derive a framework *from* the things in themselves.

The *topography* of contemporary architecture is the pursuit of a knowledge of architecture on the basis of its representation. Topography is the representation of place that reveals the knowledge of the place not as a type or class but as the place itself. Topography is geographical, but it can also be architectural. Places are physical, but they can also be mental. Such places are particular, singular, and their description should not eradicate their individuality. Topography, then, is the representation of the particular, but it is a form of representation that articulates rather than depicts: it reveals multiple topographies, rather than representing or reproducing one in the manner of a graphic simulacrum.

If this book does not have recourse to images, other than those conceptual scribbles with which certain contemporary architects have sketched out the intentions underlying their projects, it is because the topographical representation to which the title of the book alludes is primarily concerned with mental sites, those places in the mind where works of architecture install themselves. The objective addressed by the different chapters of this book is the articulation of these places by means of historical references and the interweaving play of thought, art, and culture within which works of architecture find their emplacement. The task that I believe needs undertaking is that of constructing these places, deconstructing them, revealing the origin and intention of their appearance with no other aim than that of drawing on the topographical map the contours, curves, levels, azimuths, and orientations that are necessary for a description at once analytical and intentional.

To propose a topography is to reject a topology. It is to consider that an understanding of contemporary architecture is not a question of *logos*, of universal ideas, but of *graphē*, of writings, of conventional and logical artifices by means of which a knowledge of the particular objects, of the architectures and the architects of the present moment, may hope to become more veridical.

What makes it possible to delimit the specific condition of each individual, subject, or work of art is its *differences*. Knowledge of the same permits only tautology. The possibility of being able to attribute particular characteristics to a given situation or object is founded on difference. Recognition of difference leads to the affirmation of the plural. A plural culture is one that makes of differences its profile, its distinctive outline, its characteristic feature. To approach the description of the current situation of contemporary architecture as a question of differences means taking plurality not only as a starting point but as a multiplicity within which to situate any segment of this contemporary reality.

As against the preoccupation with the autonomous discourse of architecture characteristic of structuralist thinking, the texts that make up the present volume propose a break with any watertight compartmentalization. All spaces are contaminated. Every precinct has doors and windows that communicate with other precincts and spaces. The explication of architecture exclusively in terms of architecture itself is a slack excuse, an attempt to deny the evidence of much broader relationships.

This book sets out to draw each particular situation by means of maps that, alongside architecture, include philosophy, the visual arts, literature, and cinema. This is not to assume, however, that reality is stratified, and that for each level of architectonic event there is a corresponding and analogous level in philosophy or art. Nothing could be further from my convictions than a universal homogenization of this kind. What I have tried to put forward is a sense that differences are perceived more clearly the closer the relative positions of the objects of comparison, while variables and forms of relationship are established between apparently unconnected positions and situations. That polymorphism which we necessarily employ in attacking the products of architecture, art, and culture presents us in the end with a world of figures in which any kind of provisional rhetoric will enable us to unlock the closed boxes of objects that are autonomous only in appearance.

Critical endeavor is creative to the extent that it gives rise to connections, analogies, circuits, or lines that not only might otherwise have gone unnoticed, but would have been impossible to recognize in the absence of the differential mechanism. What produces consciousness and thus the possibility of judgment is the extension of the lines of force that run from the interior of a place or an object over great distances to exogenous relations by means of which contrasts are made evident and new interactive networks unfolded, through which the delivery of information entirely overturns clichés or commonplaces; that is to say, established places.

In writing this introductory text, I am still wrestling with the impression made upon me by the recent news of the death of Gilles Deleuze. If the essays that make up this volume represent to a considerable extent an effort to break away from the rigidity of structuralist thinking, it must be obvious that this is due, in my case, to the intellectual stimulus provided by Deleuze. If in the course of the pages that follow there is an attempt at constructing an extemporary interpretive framework, as if it were a matter of building a series of platforms from which to monitor reality from multiple angles and perspectives, this is yet another attitude learned from the author of *Différence et Répétition*. If one of the recurring attempts throughout the different texts takes the form of a coining, a decanting, a manipulating of concepts and images employed like tools in the task of exploring in greater depth the complexity of the contemporary panorama, this is also owing to the French philosopher. Despite my very evident debt to Deleuze's thinking, however, I would like to distance myself unambiguously from those who in recent years have instrumentalized his thought. A certain fashion, first in Europe and then in America, has seized upon the dazzling images of his thought, either as forms to be directly visualized in new architectures or as verbal metaphors with which to beautify a conventional, if not vulgar, way of thinking.

A second philosophical influence over my work runs parallel to Deleuze's influence: the essays in this collection make frequent reference to the phenomenological thought that dominated the European scene in the 1950s. In opposition to the mechanistic psychologism of the great masters of modern architecture, yet equally in opposition to the structuralism of the 1960s, this book seeks to recover phenomenology's active engagement with things in themselves, as well as its deployment of a method grounded in the description of intentionalities with no claims to objectivity. Against the dogmatism of those who construct systems, and equally against the nihilism of those who believe that the only possible activity is to undo the entire constitution of reality, phenomenology first of all represented phenomenology as such, and then, as a hermeneutics, the need to analyze and simultaneously interpret discourse: two functions of a single intellectual process.

I am aware that by declaring a parallel interest in Deleuze and in the phenomenological tradition I am committing, as regards philosophical families, a serious crime against the canons of coherence. I have no difficulty in appreciating the enormous distance that separates Edmund Husserl and his followers' idealism from the materialist empiricism on which Deleuze draws in his finest readings of David Hume and Henri Bergson. Nevertheless, what makes it possible to reconcile the two sensibilities is a series of features that, as noted by the phenomenologists of the fifties and also by such architects as Aldo van Eyck and Ernesto Rogers, gave rise to a certain pluralism, to the priority of descriptive over normative thought, and to a recognition of the need to make thinking more an original construction than a dogmatic repetition. A primarily positivist attitude prevails in both camps—an attentiveness to the formal, eidetic dimension of our understanding—which builds more than one bridge between the poststructuralists' awareness of flows, energies, and displacements and the ontological search for intentionalities—the signification and meaning of consciousness, in short, of knowing.

The idea that architecture, practical knowledge, can and should be understood within this framework of relationships is not, in my opinion, a diversionary move into remote problems. Nevertheless, it is clearly the case that the practice of architecture is very often executed in an intuitive, inexplicit manner, and may even be guided by reasoning of an entirely different nature from those outlined in the pages of this book. From beginning to end, architecture is a text that needs to be deciphered, unraveled; one that, beyond the process of its production, moves toward a vanishing point that completely escapes its specific concrete origin.

This is not exactly a book with which to *make* architecture, nor even a book with which to separate the wheat from the chaff (to employ an ingenuous interpretation of how criticism might be described). For Deleuze, art—and architecture, an art to which he almost never made explicit reference—is a deterritorializing energy; that is to say, a vector that shatters the solipsism of a rule or the limits of topographical description in order to escape beyond the reach of any definitive localization. The project of a topography of contemporary architecture, or any topography, is an impossible task. The task of criticism is a labor of Sisyphus. Every effort at capturing the aesthetic potential of the artwork is condemned to ultimate sterility. Reality will always be more potent than thought. That is the passionate paradox from which this book stems.

Barcelona
November 1995

The role of architectural criticism has varied substantially over the course of the twentieth century. The activity of criticism occupies a specific place in relation to architectural production and to the cultural evaluation made of this production, but is itself something not well defined. Quite the reverse: *one* if we analyze the forms that architectural criticism has taken from the time of the avant-garde up to the present day, we find changing situations and relationships between the production and consumption of architecture, with the critics reacting to these changes by positioning themselves in a variety of ways.

Topographies of Contemporary Architecture

The modern movement opened with the architect and the critic in tight alliance. Critics coined a whole series of new concepts precisely in order to legitimate the new architecture. From Adolf Behne to Sigfried Giedion or Bruno Zevi, critics committed themselves to furthering the project that the architects of the avant-garde sought to put into practice. They were neither opposed to it nor detached from it, off to one side on the margins. Instead, their discourse was consistently aimed at manifesting the new values contained within the new architecture; this was, wherever possible, a discourse that aspired to a generalization of its criteria, with the aim of establishing a doctrine that would go hand in hand with the work of the project. These critics' task was to convince a culture not prepared for such things of the newness, goodness, and appropriateness of the new discoveries. Their writing frequently declared itself to be a historical discourse that set out to explain, as an urgent necessity, the process that had led from the classical tradition to that "new tradition" of which Giedion spoke. There was no separation between practice and theory: the objectives of practicing architects and critics coincided; each was a stimulus to the other; they justified one another through the pursuit of a historical, cultural, and technical legitimacy that would make the new architecture a most valuable contribution to society and to culture as a whole.

The situation of critical suspension that came into being in the prevailing climate following World War II, serving as a corollary to the individualistic, decentered thought of existentialism, led to a loss of trust between practicing architects and critics. Their distance from one another ultimately resulted in an atmosphere of mutual ignorance and alienation.

This perplexing scenario, to which we shall return in due course, was followed by a new conception of criticism as radical critique. If architectural practice had taken the path of self-sufficiency, internal reflection, and tradition, radical criticism was to deploy itself as the global condemnation of this ideological construction. During the 1960s and 1970s we experienced a continuing series of sweeping disqualifications of the whole of architectural activity: architecture is a discourse of constant mystification; the messages of functionality, public service, honesty, rationality, and constructive logic are fraudulent; the words of architects are the products of a rhetoric of deception; they promise what they cannot deliver, proposing unattainable utopias and impossible models of living; architecture has become the lackey of the mythologizing forces in society; capitalism has an intrinsic need to cover over reality with discourses full of tricks, deceptions, and manipulations that conceal the truly perverse nature of the processes underlying the construction of spaces for public and private life; the critic must be a lucid, distant conscience, set apart from the rhetorical vacuousness of these discourses. The critique of architectural ideology was a call for criticism to constitute itself as accusation, unmasking, and negative judgment. Distanced from the practice of architecture, the critic both repudiated and disowned it. But criticism did not stop there: it rose up against architecture. The critic is not a natural judge, free of all prejudice. He or she is the voice of the other, of that to which architecture is opposed. Instead of promoting a particular attitude, he or she disqualifies all attitudes in the name of a global mistrust of everything for which architectural discourse stands.

The present situation seems to have lost the rigor and certainty of radicalism without having established any new accord or collaboration with practice. This is the outcome of an intellectual situation in which there are no generally accepted systems either of values or political principles on the basis of which architecture can be judged. Meanwhile, architecture proves itself to be hesitant, doubt-ridden, and far from prolific when it comes to rationalizing its proposals. The proliferation of declarations of intent is accompanied by a dearth of well-founded reasoning. Present-day works of architecture and their authors reveal desires, intentions, but limited projects. Contemporary criticism cannot approach them with either the strength of an organized army or the conclusive logic of a clear division between architecture's actors and critics. More than bodies of theory, what we are faced with are situations, de facto projects that have sought to find their consistency in the specific conditions of each event. A diffuse heterogeneity pervades the world of the architectural object. Each scheme emerges from the conjuncture of partial, fragmentary discourses. It seems more and more that we are confronted not so much with a work of architecture as a point of intersection, the interaction of forces and energies proceeding from diverse locations whose momentary deflagration explains a concrete and particular architectural situation, action, and production.

In our current condition of epistemological poststructuralism and political nihilism, it is impossible for criticism to be anything other than a provisional system. From a multiplicity of platforms, criticism today can undertake the production of maps or descriptions which, like topographical charts, reveal the complexity of a territory—its form the result of geological agents operating in silence on an apparently immobile mass that is nevertheless cut through by currents, flows, changes, and interactions that give rise to incessant mutations.

The explication of architecture is not some arborescent endeavor, comparable to the branches of a tree growing out of a common trunk and nourished through its roots from a particular soil. Architecture is not a tree but an event, resulting from the intersection of forces capable of situating an object that is partially signifying, contingent. Criticism is thus not the recognition or manifestation of branches but is itself a construct, purposefully produced to cast light on that situation, as a means of drawing the topography of that point where a certain architecture has been produced.

The purpose of this book is none other than to undertake just such a critical construct: an outline of the contemporary situation, drawn with a mechanism whose instruments stem from a variety of sources. Starting from the conviction that there are no fixed criteria from which to approach works of architecture, either of the present or the past, this exercise will attempt to find analogies between the current situation and that of western architecture after World War II. This hypothesis clearly does not posit that we are once again at the same point as before, or that history repeats itself. Historical conditions never repeat themselves, but analogies can offer an eminently viable means of signaling structures of behavior and signification by which they render themselves mutually intelligible, precisely on the basis of their similarities and differences.

In attempting to demonstrate certain connections and transformations, I hope to establish both the paradigms of these respective situations and the criteria that have proved effective in revealing these two key moments in the architecture of the twentieth century. For example, chapter 3, which explores the notion of existentialist architecture, transfers to architecture a term that served to describe a whole complex of characteristic features of the culture of the fifties, both in Europe and in the United States. This transfer allows for the possibility of capturing those shared features in the architecture of that time in such a way that the same set of aspirations and problems, conceptions of the world and of the subject, may describe the philosophy and literature of those years as well as outline their architectural topography.

We are not today in the same situation. But the return of the subject, of the psychology of global perception, of the experience of the void, of the inevitable presences of function and of place, of movement, and of the absence of any kind of limit appear to have established new formulations in the present context. To the will to silence and the intention of avoiding any kind of articulated explanation, criticism today, as in the past, opposes its project of constructing a discourse, of installing a mechanism with which to capture those features, profiles, attitudes, and values that constitute an essential part of what appears time and time again in contemporary projects.

My proposal for comparison consists of looking on the one hand at a selection of buildings such as the Farnsworth house by Ludwig Mies van der Rohe (1945–1950); the Yale Art Gallery in New Haven by Louis Kahn (1951–1953); the church in Imatra by Alvar Aalto (1956–1959); the Ugalde house in Caldetes by J. Antonio Coderch (1950–1951); and the Borsalino apartments in Alessandria by Ignazio Gardella (1950–1952). These are all buildings constructed during the fifties, by architects whose capability is beyond question. Each of these projects presents itself as neither more nor less than the response determined by certain specific conditions, without any kind of universality or the application of any shared, single body of knowledge, theory, or linguistic repertoire.

Alongside this series of five buildings from the fifties, I propose another selection of five buildings from the eighties. These are the commercial building in Kyoto by Tadao Ando (1983–1990); the Ricola warehouses in Basel by Jacques Herzog and Pierre de Meuron (1986–1987); the Schnabel house in Santa Monica by Frank Gehry (1988–1990); the auditorium in Salamanca by Juan Navarro Baldeweg (1989–1992); and the Faculty of Architecture in Oporto by Alvaro Siza (1988–1992).

One common concern manifests itself in all five of the works from the fifties: not only to adapt the form to the clear definition of a program, but to make the functional program underpin the building's form. Discussing functionalism as a doctrine will not serve to clarify this common denominator. Edward de Zurko's famous book *Origins of Functionalist Theory*, published in the late 1950s, makes precisely the point that functionalism in architecture is as old as architecture itself. Although de Zurko appeared to be primarily concerned with annulling the specific character of the functionalist position in those years, what actually concerned him as a theoretician was the historical legitimation of a certain tendency. Functional, he felt, was not exactly synonymous with useful, practical, or efficient. He argued that a building's functional quality should be made explicit, communicable, and easily recognizable. The added value of architecture should be derived from its novel or multiple uses, and consequently architecture should visually order itself on the basis of the programmatic order of its functions. The technical core and the transparent space of the Farnsworth house, Kahn's serving and served spaces, the anchoring of the volumes of the Imatra church, the morphological ruptures of the Ugalde house, or the slight gestural movements of the Borsalino apartments all clearly and perceptibly designate different spaces for different uses. Together, they constitute an architecture born out of abstraction that sought, in the particularity of each program, a ground for its formal justification. Zoned, organic, and constructive, these buildings' functional resources articulated their architectural form and expression.

In light of de Zurko's description of functionalism as ingenuous doctrine and expositional mechanism, today's built message seems to communicate itself in a far more mediated fashion. Relying on the notion of character and the mediation of images—derived above all from sculpture and the visual arts—today's built form is deployed by

Jungian archetypes: the elementary silhouette of the house as natural notion; the skin as enveloping any monumental, public, significant space; basic geometries as references to the congenital, the essential; and materials as a return to the source. All of these features, already experienced in minimalism in the plastic arts, would seem to constitute the support for such architects as Gehry, Siza, Ando, Herzog and de Meuron, and Navarro Baldeweg. The object is no longer to render apparent the practical utility of the building; rather, its justification as form is based on appeals to the deep structures of our psyche, evoking these by means of archetypal images through which architectural character is revealed in a way that is as powerful as it is anterior to any logical or narrative discourse.

We are evidently dealing here with a displacement from the surface to the depths, but what is preserved in both situations is the framing of the pursuit of meaning in terms of a particular, individual code, specific to each case. Our concern here is not with the use of stylistic codes that render a building recognizable as a particular instance of a common language, but with the search, in each case and for each work, for the presence and the manifestation that are inherently proper to it.

The uncertainty with which modern architecture broached the question of the formal definition of the object was met, during the crisis of the fifties, with the pantheistic response of the dissolution of the object in the landscape. The renewal of interest in the picturesque tradition, as developed by Nikolaus Pevsner in a number of patently doctrinal articles, attempted to resolve the modern experience of the inconsistency of objects as such by reducing as much as possible all distinctions between the built and the natural through means of integration, continuity, connection between interior and exterior, and adaptation.

These were the catchwords with which dematerialization, fragmentation, and camouflage— the recurring strategies for the new architecture —were explained. For the five 1950s buildings of our selection, as for so many others, these concerns were understood both as positive values and as a necessary abrogation that architecture made of its own presence in the interest of landscape as continuum—a continuum in which architecture was to be no more than one amongst a multiplicity.

Today's landscape hardly constitutes a background into which the architectural object might be thought of as inserting, or integrating, or diffusing itself. Powerful processes of what Gilles Deleuze has called deterritorialization situate today's architectural objects in non-places, in non-landscapes. Contemporary architectures make their appearance *ex abrupto*, taking us by surprise. Their presence is not connected to a place. Our reception of them is almost always mediated or mediatized by photographic, video, and computerized images, by possible views, and by the disconnection between the built and what goes on around it. It might almost be said that we are now at the opposite pole from the picturesque integration of the fifties, were it not for the fact that integration and estrangement must be considered as two faces of the same problematic coin. The fifties' pantheistic fusion with the landscape and today's isolated stupor of the object both serve to demonstrate that the architectural object no longer establishes a stable and hierarchical relationship between itself and its surroundings. Quite the opposite: the mediated—in both senses of the term—condition of architecture leads it into a relationship with its surroundings, which is to say with the world, that is always adventitious, improper, extrinsic. An organicist pantheism has given way to a rootless atheism. In both of these situations, architecture

cannot conceal the depth of its wound: the absence of a felicitous relationship with the territory, with nature, and with life.

The Gestalt psychologism that impregnates all conceptions of form at the origins of the architecture of the modern movement undertakes its displacement from the simply visual to the synesthetically complex precisely in the culture of the postwar period. Maurice Merleau-Ponty's *Phenomenologie de la perception* of 1945 offers a synthetic summary of a body of research based on studies of both the structure of behavior and the primacy of perception. This research displaced the merely visual, replacing it with the idea that our experience of the world around us comes from the body in its totality: spatio-temporal, sexual, mobile, and expressive. The visual-tactile dichotomy posited by Aloïs Riegl in the early years of the century in order to analyze the various different orders of aesthetic experience was converted by the phenomenologists into a much more general, more basic theory. Even the aesthetic was thus to be understood as that which was connected not with artistic perception but, in a much wider sense, with interactions of every kind between the self and the world.

These ideas were reflected in the architecture of the time in its abandonment of traditional artistic discourse and its preoccupation with the global phenomena of perception of all kinds. Team X's debates and Art Brut's or Cobra's creative groupings reflected a more general cultural and academic interest in archaic, primitive cultures. These various forays into cultural anthropology helped to bring about a crisis that not only swept away the academic separation between art and everyday life, but also put an end to a conception of architecture's goal as the production of effects linked to a concept of beauty constituting a higher order of the formally aesthetic.

The crisis and the critique of the fifties in the field of aesthetics were not to be assuaged by the frustrated renaissance of classical forms in the seventies. It is quite apparent that the effect sought by Mies, Kahn, Aalto, Coderch, or Gardella in their work had nothing to do with any pursuit of the idea of the beautiful such as we continue to find, for example, in Le Corbusier. When the relationship between the subject and the world has turned problematic, not even the empirical inquiries of phenomenological research are of any avail. We live today in the estrangement between self and others, between the self and the world, on the margins even between self and individual. Our perception is not structuring but nomadic. The experience of one's own body and of what is external to it is made up of heterogeneous ingredients, of atoms that do not compose molecules, of portions that fail to fit together. This erratic, nomadic perception of reality is such a characteristic feature of our crisis that architecture manifests it in a multitude of ways. It is not only fragmentation that fractures projects into particles difficult to recompose. It is also the fact that the unfinished, the partial, and the cumulative have become predominant in a way of working that presents itself as incapable of proposing any higher level of integration.

Accumulation, reiteration, difference, and disconnection are some of the substantives most frequently repeated in discussion of architectures such as those we have proposed as representative of our present situation. It is not only that the sources of our relationship with the world have extended and multiplied. It is also the case that, as they have done so, the ideals of integration, coherence, and synthesis that had presided over the artistic production of the past have become patently unattainable. With the disappearance of these ideals, the practice of architecture presents itself as an undertaking that is humble, fragile, a permanent approximation, insuperably provisional.

Among the ideals of modern architecture, one of those most celebrated by its exegetes was its incorporation of movement into what had been, throughout its history, by definition static and immovable. The architecture of this era of Einsteinian relativity was described as embodying movement, and therefore time as a fourth dimension. Put more precisely, what this meant was that architecture promoted movement through its interior and exterior—architecture became above all a space for mobility, a container in which movement was prefigured. One consequence of this theoretical construct was that architecture generated an inevitable sense of void. The architectures we have taken as examples of the critical situation following World War II invariably present themselves as voids, negative molds for our experience of permanent mobility. While this architecture was negative in the sense of prioritizing space over form, it was positive in the sense of suggesting an atmosphere of possibility—an empty stage upon which a new, modern mode of living was to be experienced or enacted.

The spatiality that seemed to have established itself as a hegemonic category in the fifties has been radically transformed in our time, converting the vacancy of its lines of virtual construction into pure absence. While the void previously promised possibility, today it reflects the emptiness of everyday life. Rather than providing a stage upon which a drama is played, architecture has become a documentary window, revealing our own reality. Terms employed in the description of contemporary practice—transparency, dilation, absence of limits, spatial interconnection—suggest that architecture acts more as a negative form than as the proposition of any precise figurative content. Never before has architecture been interpreted as the testimony of an emigration, as the abandoned precincts of gods and men who are no longer with us. The intimacy, loneliness, and reality of the void are no longer papered over; instead, the Nietzschean philosophy of desertion, abandonment, and twilight seems to find a clear and deliberate echo in the most sensitive works of our age.

The space that once upon a time was capable of occasioning for the user or the observer experiences of the void, the abstract synesthesia of dynamico-temporal perception, seems to have become less compulsive, less projective. Instead of giving rise to new stimuli, the architecture of today seems to reiterate, in a weary voice, that these innovations and those excitations are no longer possible, or are, in any case, futile. A sometimes nihilistic, sometimes realistic wind blows through present-day architecture, sweeping away the gestures, the words, and the images that the architecture generated during the crisis climate of the 1950s could still posit. That moment was underpinned by the pathos of insecurity, of the horrors of the war, and of the contradictions of social life, and was accordingly cushioned by an architecture that promised an optimistic alternative.

In the architecture of Ando or Navarro Baldeweg, time has come to a stop and passions seem to be stilled. There is no longer even a subject to shout and gesticulate. With the disappearance of the gods, of myths, of hopes, and of dreams, architecture has also emptied itself of individualism and subjectivity. Clearly there is no collective voice to take its place. It is still more evident that the sensibility of the best artists captures nothing other than a third person who is neither me nor you, nor him nor her. The quality of the work of art, and thus of architecture, can no longer be gauged either by any objective standard or by the forces of invention, innovation, or the subject's singularity. The fitting silence of today's architecture is one that corresponds, as in the obsessive images of science fiction, to the surface of the moon: lunar spaces in which recognition of the topography affords us a knowledge that is as disturbing as it is useless. The topography of contemporary architecture that might be drawn up by criticism today is one of desolate landscapes, of still lifes in which the void is an intensity to be resolved simultaneously in the imagination and the memory. This contemporary architecture of the void provokes, rather than soothes.

There would be little point in performing a diagnosis of the present situation if we did not possess some shared idea of health. The sole task of criticism is to make measurements and determine levels of the state of things as we find them. Drawing one of many possible relief maps of this empty territory in which architecture finds itself makes public and collective a situation that demands to be lived as something individual and private. Publishing such a cartography of present-day architecture offers the only possibility of submitting it to the judgment of somebody, of some public, at some time, in some place. Each reader will accordingly chart his or her own cartographic course, cutting through these pages to reveal yet another possible architectural relief or event.

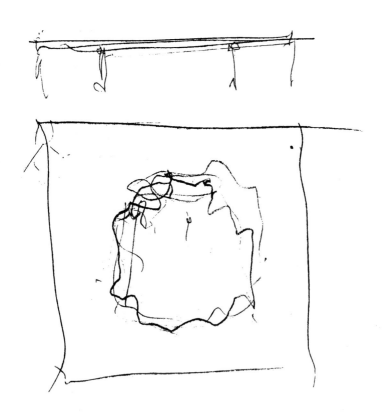

During the course of the identity crisis that beset the modern movement in the 1960s, one of the theoretical tasks was the committed reappraisal of the work of the masters of modern architecture. This cultural operation began at a moment of crisis not only in architecture but in the visual arts in general. The *two* postpainterly movement saw the emergence of alternative and radical lines of working. Among these, minimalism and pop art constituted two opposing lines of exploration, both originating from dissatisfaction with expressionism's subjectivism and the formalism imposed by painting's conventions. The question of signification was a central concern for both pop and minimalist artists. For the minimalists, the object was to return to a zero point, a writing *degree zero*, to recall Roland Barthes's well-known text of 1953, on the basis of which to construct, painstakingly, a number of minimum aesthetic significations. For pop art, in its symmetrical and opposing way, the desired signification was the imitation of models established by the tradition or in the

Mies van der Rohe and Minimalism

new repertoires—iconic, widespread, and popular—disseminated by the new mass media.

In architecture, there was clearly a parallel phenomenon. Faced with the no longer tenable clichés of the modern tradition, there were those who sought, through a return to origins—to the pure wellsprings of enlightened architecture, or to the purism of the modern movement—to restore the essential words and founding gestures of the language of architecture. Others, in marked contrast, believed that they saw in the diffusion of the popular or in the prestige of classical architecture the power to renew signification. Curiously, the return to Mies van der Rohe that began in the 1980s and continues today among certain practitioners, in academia, and in exhibitions was undertaken from both of these standpoints—two points of view that were not always well defined, but were often held simultaneously.

It is apparent now that the problem of signification prompted a powerful need to read the classical architectural tradition into Mies's architecture, and that this need gave rise to a false and mistaken reading of his work. Claiming Mies had a classical basis in his apprenticeship to Peter Behrens and in his Berlin-nurtured sympathy for the work of Karl Friedrich Schinkel, revisionists have put Mies forward in recent years as an atypical master of the modern movement clad in classical tradition, despite the apparent modernity of his glass and steel buildings. It is now time to publicly denounce this enterprise. It too closely resembles what has also been attempted with Frank Lloyd Wright and Le Corbusier: all of these endeavors reveal the desire of architects and critics to find a consistent signification in the work of an architect whose solutions, duly standardized and manipulated, had become the most rhetorically representative commonplace of commercial architecture.

Yet the classicism to be found in certain of Mies's buildings hardly constitutes an argument capable of explaining the aesthetic intensity of his work. The references to Doric temples and to the Erectheum, the parallels with Schinkel's Altes Museum and the Neue Wache, the surprising views of the Barcelona pavilion through Ionic columns, or the carving up of the columns of the Neue Nationalgalerie in Berlin as a redesigning of the classical orders all correspond to an anxious search for meaning through imitation and classical mimesis. These arguments constitute an ideological operation that is difficult to justify on the basis of Mies's attitude, his writings, and the body of his work as a whole.

Mies's work was not born of the desire to recreate a permanent, transhistorical nature based on the classical orders and their grammar. Nor is it licit to think of Mies, after the manner of Duchamp, as the author of a series of architectural *readymades*, products of some kind of modern nominalism where the redundancy of the classical icons employed would guarantee the meaning of the work of architecture. In his 1984 study of Duchamp, *Nominalisme pictural*, the art theorist Thierry de Duve coined the expression *pictorial nominalism* to describe the conventional procedure by which aesthetically nonsignificant objects—the *Fountain*, for example—are transformed into works of art. This nominalism, based on the de facto acceptance of the artistic status of any object whatsoever, takes the place of Platonic essentialism. Order, obtained between nature and art, in the harmony of a unique cosmos, guarantees the profound signification of the work of art. The semantic procedure is based on the imitative condition—*ars simiae naturae*, art imitates nature—intrinsic to the classical modus operandi. Architectural nominalism, conventionally, makes use of the classical as a sign, as a surface display denoting the artistic, in the same way that so-called postmodern architecture, in Charles Jencks's version of it, has contrived to do ad nauseam.

In Mies, however, there is no reference to the totality of the cosmos from which classical art constructed meaning, orders, types, proportions, and perspective. It makes no sense, then, to turn Mies into the last classicist. Yet neither is there a pop Mies, capable of freely appropriating the significations of the classical tradition with the cool daring of a bank robber, a kidnapper. On the contrary, in the construction of a degree zero of the architectural text the procedure is entirely different.

Mies's work is developed not out of images but out of materials—materials in the strongest sense of the word; that is, the matter from which objects are constructed. This matter is abstract, general, geometrically cut, smooth, and polished, but it is also material that is substantial, tangible, and solid. And at the same time, it implies a wider materiality that takes in the gravity and weight of the elements of construction, the tensions in their static behavior, their hardness or fragility, and the material artifice of the technology that prepares and handles the elements from which the building is raised. This is a materialism, finally, that sets out from the origin of the material problems of lighting, air conditioning, sealing of the outer skin, and the satisfactory functioning of the building in relation to the use for which it was designed. The whole tremendous body of innovation in Mies derives neither from imitation nor from the abstract discourse of concepts of space, light, or territory. In Mies, the realities are, from the very outset, material for the work of architecture. His calls to understand architecture solely as building, as *Bauen*, are no mere lip service to a fashionable functionalism, but rather are proof that for the creator of the Tugendhat house, the perceptual conditions established by the materiality of the building form the very origins of its spiritual signification. It is only by way of the material conditions that we can arrive at "the forces which act in their interior" and the "authentic field of actuation which is, without a doubt, that of signification," as Mies explained in 1953.

Of course, the relationship that is established between the materiality of the architectural object and its reception as spiritual signification does not, for Mies, take place in some previously elaborated tissue of abstract elements such as rhythm, balance, proportion, and measure. These values are, in any event, an outcome. To put it another way, the architect does not adapt the forms of his materials to previously established laws or conventions that have to be imitated or reproduced.

Our relationship with architecture is immediate. The work of modern art, as Deleuze and Guattari observe in their 1991 book *Qu'est-ce que la philosophie?*, is a block of sensations, that is to say a compound of perceptions and effects (*percepts et affects*). Such sensations do not act as metaphors, transferring us to other objects or images serving as points of reference. The material and its durability are what support and produce both the perceptions we receive by means of our senses and the effects that are neither merely subjective nor to be considered pure reactions on the part of the individual confronted with the work of art. The radical architecture of Mies is a consolidated, permanent block for the production of sensations, through which materials pass and concepts are reached.

The abstract condition of the Miesian sensibility reinforces the transition from sensation to perception and from perception to concept, a concept that has nothing to do with science or philosophy, that steers well clear of the dangers associated with so-called conceptual art. Through the extreme dematerialization of its messages, the latter tended, in effect, toward pure information, toward taxonomy, toward the formulation of general aims and projects. Mies's art, like the work of Donald Judd or Dan Flavin, has a material component that delimits it. The concrete materiality common to these works makes them not general but particular: they are not the expression of a general idea but tangible physical objects, the producers of perceptions and effects.

It is wrong to think of the architecture of Mies as a stage, even as an empty one. This metaphor, as it has been used by Manfredo Tafuri and certain of his disciples in reference to the Barcelona pavilion, betrays once again the modernity of Mies's work by reducing it to a framework—the stage—that is by definition a previously determined visual convention. To speak of the empty stage is to see the perceptual emissions constituted by Mies's buildings as the last redoubt of the work of art as representation. Yet modern sensibility has abandoned this procedure. Since the empiricism of the eighteenth century, since David Hume and Edmund Burke, since Uvedale Price and Richard Payne Knight, the aesthetic experience has been the unexpected commotion provoked by a course pursued at random, by an accumulation of images, by an excess of stimulations.

In his essay of 1931, "A Small History of Photography," Walter Benjamin said, "The cinema provides material for collective, simultaneous reception, just as architecture has always done." In Mies's work, the perception that we are offered presupposes neither point of view nor order of reading nor hierarchy. Modern vision, which photography developed, has resulted, as Paul Virilio suggests, in the disappearance not only of spatial distance but also of distance in time. There is nothing fortuitous about Mies's interest in photomontage and in exercising control over the photographs reproduced in his books; photographs, it should be noted, for which all notions of stage setting or theatricality prove entirely inadequate.

In the same way, to speak of context in the work of Mies is to introduce another inadequate, inappropriate conceptual paradigm. His works of architecture were not produced in relation to the context, nor did they constitute a commentary on or mimesis of the place in which they were situated. Once again, looking at things in this way is a trick whose purpose is to carry Mies's work beyond the architect's own intentions. In the words of Harold Rosenberg, minimalist works of art "affirm the independent existence of the artistic object as significative in itself" rather than in relation to works from the past, to social ideas, or to individual emotions.

This isolated, autonomous condition of the aesthetic experience has some bearing on the self-referential character of Mies's architecture. With Mies, architecture is never a monument. It is not a monument in the strict etymological sense of that word: a work that refers to, recalls, something outside itself, such as an event, a moment in history, the community, its origins, or certain civic or moral values. In his writings, Mies appeals time and again to the spiritual signification that the work of architecture ought to attain. In his excellent exegesis of the sources of Mies's thinking, Fritz Neumeyer has underlined the importance to Mies of the phenomenological tradition of the followers of Max Scheler. Romano Guardini and Paul Landsberg are two thinkers, contemporary with Mies, whose influence on him seems beyond doubt. Perhaps, however, Neumeyer might have laid greater emphasis on the fact that there was a religious problem occupying a central place in the concerns of each of these thinkers. Guardini, a Catholic priest, endlessly sought out meaningful relations between human beings, things, and technology. He tried to reconstruct meaning in a post-Nietzschean world in which not only God was dead, but the Hegelian proclamation of the death of art was at the roots of the activities of the avant-garde. Guardini, whose most developed thought on aesthetics can be found in his texts on liturgy and sacred symbols, meditated throughout his life on transcendent significance as something stemming from, but superseding, the concrete materiality of the objects, gestures, and words of human life. Landsberg, who was a Jew by birth and who died in a concentration camp in 1944, was a friend of Emmanuel Mounier and the French personalists, and he devoted his working life to elaborating a philosophical anthropology, a body of thought that was to reconstruct a place for humanity, human production, and interpersonal relations.

This is the context in which Mies developed his self-referential conception of the work of art. Perhaps the difference between Mies's use of the notion and that of the minimalists derives precisely from the degree to which this self-reference is held as being open or closed in relation to other values. For the minimalists of the 1960s and later, the work neither appeals to nor evokes anything other than itself. It partakes of the pure randomness inherited from Stéphane Mallarmé and the final silence of Kasimir Malevich. The work of art is self-referential because it begins and ends in itself and explains only its own materiality, factuality, and obviousness. In Mies there is much of this same spirit, which preserves the work of architecture from any temptation to make it the vehicle for some other signification or the expression of some other content. In Mies, too, the architecture refers to itself. It makes of its own presence the primordial act of its signification. But in Mies there is an ethical project that is carried out precisely in the work. The entire debate regarding technology in the period between the wars was an ethical debate. Whether the author was Oswald Spengler or Martin Heidegger, Thomas Mann or Ernst Jünger, the reflections on technology and its products were framed from an ethical viewpoint within the perspective of the reconstruction following in the wake of Nietzschean nihilism. Analyses of the differences between *technē* and *poiēsis* in Greek thought, such as were being undertaken by Werner Jaeger, were born of a prevalent preoccupation of the time, from which Mies was by no means immune. The reconsideration of medieval aesthetics, in which production and meaning were perceived as indivisible, provided the thinkers mentioned above, and Mies among them, with an indisputable point of reference. The autonomy of the work of architecture, the project of making of it once again a "solid and enduring compound," as Paul Cézanne said of his project for painting, is the very heart of Mies's work. Architecture should not be solipsistic, closed in on itself, complacently satisfied with its own interests, nor purely empirical, the "I do not seek, I find" of Pablo Picasso. The Miesian project in architecture is inscribed within a wider ethical project in which the architect's contribution to society is made precisely by means of the transparency, economy, and obviousness of his architectural proposals. His is the contribution of truth, of honesty. That is his message.

The year 1968 marked, symbolically, the end of the modern movement and the explosion of postmodern culture. At that time minimalism, as a current, had already been given not only its name but also its definition through the writings of Clement Greenberg, Barbara Rose, Harold Rosenberg, Irving Sandler, and Richard Wollheim, among others. It was the year in which the Neue Nationalgalerie opened in Berlin, the last of Mies's buildings to be completed in the architect's lifetime. And it was at this moment that Gilles Deleuze published his most important book of philosophy, *Différence et répétition*. "I think we will have this work going round our heads for a long time to come. Perhaps one day the century will be Deleuzean," Michel Foucault prophesied.

To cite Deleuze's text here is relevant because it contains a figurative thought capable of formulating the evident nexus between the aesthetic experience of minimalism and the work of Mies. Conceived as a way of breaking away from the rigidity of structuralist thinking, and at the same time escaping the pure decomposition of the post-Nietzschean carnival, Deleuze's text establishes the bases for a process of signification and construction of meaning grounded in the imbalance that introduces repetition and difference into the monist idea of the same and the uniform. Repetition as innovation, as a mechanism of liberation, of life and death; repetition as will, as the opposite of the laws of nature; repetition as a new morality beyond habit and memory; repetition that only attains tension and creativity with the fissures of difference, with disequilibrium, innovation.

The explanation of
the development of
the architecture of the
modern movement has
always suffered from a
considerable conceptual
weakness. First, the pro-
tagonists of its founding
phase thought that this
development was a natural
process. This organicist
model was in due course
succeeded by a belief that *three*
what was happening, within
a supposed orthodoxy, was
no more than an expansion or
spread that extended mod-
ernism's originary principles
over new areas and new problems. Finally, an explanation in
terms of a biographical and generational vision was put forth that
envisioned modernism's advance-
ment as a relay race, in which the
second, third, and fourth generations
figured as links in a chain.

In recent years, a more radical idea
of crisis seemed to suggest that this conceptual weakness of continuity has been
broken, that the thread of this modern tradition, as Sigfried Giedion called it, has
been severed by the radicalism of those who
profoundly abhorred it, or by those who, in
seeking to reconstitute it, opted for a return to
origins, understood by some as the heroic years

of the avant-garde, by others as the no less foundational age of the Enlightenment.

Today there seems to be a real need to explore this situation of crisis in the hopes of discovering new hypotheses that avoid the trap of the logic described above. To undertake such an endeavor, it is necessary to start out from the premise that there is not *one* crisis in the architecture of the modern movement, but *many*. These different crises form part of the contradictions contained in the very idea of a coherent, unitary modern movement. Inasmuch as it proved possible to identify shared principles and methods, these were called into question from the very moment of their formulation. Rather than attempt to enumerate each and all of the crises that can be detected in modernism's architectonic culture over the last sixty years, I would like to analyze one distinct point of inflection—existentialism—in the hopes of demonstrating that changes in formal and figurative repertoires do not result from a simple mutation of gesture, but from epistemological changes that affect the culture of a specific time and so, by extension, its architecture.

I propose, then, to consider existentialism not as a strictly philosophical current but as a cultural climate that brought with it a reordering of ethical and aesthetic viewpoints, and that consequently engendered profound changes in architecture in the years following World War II. What is of interest here is the way in which a reorganization of cultural objects, resulting from an alternative conception of the individual and of society, effectively undermined modern architecture's theoretical structure, deflecting it toward different values. This shift in values was to have decisive consequences for the conceptual perspective that dominated European and American architecture during the fifties.

Dwellings

The Athens Charter of 1933 divided architectural activity into four major areas. Dwelling, recreation, work, and transportation were differentiated as distinct fields of architecture, ascribed distinct typological researches, and assigned mutually exclusive urban zones.

The destruction occasioned by World War II brought the dwelling quadrant to the fore; developing new forms of housing became a matter of urgent priority. In a manifesto published in a 1947 issue of *Baukunst und Werkform*, a highly representative group of German architects, including Max Taut, Willi Baumeister, Lilly Reich, Otto Bartning, and Max Tessenow, issued a call for architects to address fundamental necessities. The first point in this text declares: "The great cities should be rebuilt with new residential units capable of autonomous life. Only the center of the old city should acquire new life as a cultural and political heart." This clear assertion that residential building was of primary importance in the new cities, or in existing zones in need of reconstruction, was accompanied by an affirmation that was to have far-reaching aesthetic consequences: "For housing, only what is simple and valid should be pursued."

This was not an appeal to the rational, the technologically innovative, or the *Existenzminimum*, but rather a summons that adopted an entirely different set of terms. The notion of the simple and the valid constituted an appeal, in effect, to the very opposite of the new and the experimental. Endorsing a particular kind of return to origins, the signatories of this manifesto hoped to restore a grounding in experience and a restoration of the authentic.

Also in 1947, CIAM convened once again, this time in Bridgwater, England. At this meeting, Aldo van Eyck formulated a rigorous critique directed against any kind of architectural mechanization. Van Eyck's directive clearly targeted functionalism, which had until then served as a key tenet of modernism. A profound division thus appeared, separating the young architects recently incorporated into the debate on modern architecture from the more established voices of CIAM, who continued to maintain their functionalist, prewar convictions. For van Eyck, the object was not to achieve concrete, quantifiable responses to specific functional necessities; on the contrary, what was sought was an architecture that could satisfy man's emotional needs. A similar change in the tone and register of concerns is apparent in Jacob Bakema's contribution to the conference. Bakema, who was subsequently to reconstruct Rotterdam, also called for an architecture whose fundamental aim would be that of stimulating man's spiritual growth.

The terminology of existentialism—a language of humanism, emotions, spiritual growth, authenticity, and validity—had made its debut on the architectural scene. Its application within the discourse of architecture soon became abundantly evident in the texts of those authors most responsive to the new cultural climate. With them, in a slow but inexorable displacement of the coordinates within which architecture had been conceived, there began a process of conceptual reorientation that was to gain dominance in the following decade.

It was at the 1953 CIAM, in Aix-en-Provence, that this shift in values was explicitly and specifically consolidated in relation to housing. Peter and Alison Smithson, appearing at CIAM for the first time, advanced their incipient theory of urban structure: a theory that was thought out from and for housing. According to the Smithsons' logic, habitation is the paradigm of urban life. Their articulated, exponential conceptualization of urban form as originating with the house, then the street, the district, and the city abandons the quadripartite division of the city as it had been described in the Athens Charter, and places the individual at the center of the organization of the habitable space. Similarly, Josep Lluís Sert's call for the construction of millions of homes was a profession of faith not in industrialized mass production or service mechanization, but in a structure at the scale of the individual, the city dweller as subject.

At the next Congrès, held in Dubrovnik in 1956, the new key concept of identity took over the center of the architects' and urbanists' reflections. Identity assumed a primordial significance precisely because its absence was interpreted as constituting the greatest ill of the city, both actual and envisioned. These reflections on the problem of urban identity constituted a subtle yet piercing attack on the canons and criteria of the modern movement.

By the time the last CIAM was convened, in Otterlo in 1959, the change in direction had been fully consummated. The confrontation between the "young"—van Eyck, Sert, Giancarlo De Carlo, Ernesto Rogers, and the Smithsons—and the "old"—Giedion, Gropius, and Le Corbusier—was something more than a petty domestic dispute. The call for identity and the dissemination of other humanist concepts, such as core and cluster, should not be interpreted as simply a substitution of an organicist for a mechanistic metaphorical language. Over and above a certain organic formalism, inspired by models of the natural world, the core is the heart, the germinal and profound nucleus of things, while the cluster is not merely a cluster of grapes or a bunch of flowers but the gathering, the association of living beings, the interchange of vital flows in a coexistence that bestows meaning on the individual as an inseparable part of a larger human group. The fact that all of these sentiments became integral to the discussion of postwar architectural and urban reconstruction indicates not only the priority of housing as the driving force of this urban transformation, but also that during a period of at least two decades it was on the house, the dwelling, that the search for an architecture capable of responding to these demands was concentrated.

Meanwhile, similar concerns were at the heart of a different discussion regarding habitation. The widely disseminated text by Martin Heidegger, "Bauen, Wohnen, Denken," is not an esoteric meditation by a philosopher on the fringes of what was happening in postwar Europe, but a concrete response by the former rector of Freiburg to an initiative, the Darmstadt *Gespräch*, that brought together experts from a range of backgrounds to offer and consider contributions from their different fields. Heidegger's paper, delivered in 1951 and attended, we might note in passing, by José Ortega y Gasset, was published the following year in a Darmstadt journal and was subsequently included in the 1954 volume of Heidegger's *Essays and Lectures*.

What more dramatic setting than a city reduced to rubble by Allied bombing raids in the last days of the war could promote reflections directed at builders, architects, planners, and politicians? Heidegger began his address by noting the vital relevance of the housing problem, not as a theoretical question but as a task at hand, there and then physically present. But the philosopher immediately turned from the conjunctural to the essential. For Heidegger, dwelling had become problematic as such. Contemporary man no longer dwelled in a plausible and fecund relationship with the city and the world. The need to reconstruct the dwelling was not, for Heidegger, a matter of a housing shortage, but a consequence of the condition of modern man: contemporary man was stateless, without a home, without a place from which the call to dwelling could be made in any immediate manner.

For Heidegger, dwelling is a task. Mortals have to learn to dwell, and can do so immediately upon recognizing that their rootless situation must be changed. There is a way, a process, by which man should summon himself to dwell. But this process is none other than a work of construction; something that must be done, and will be done, step by step, by gathering together the necessary elements. It is for this reason that dwelling entails construction, which is the process by which man, assembled together with others, assembles things or objects. Thus dwelling, which begins as a process of putting an end to our uprootedness, ultimately leads to construction. The end of dwelling is residence, and the process of construction is thereby to erect a residence, a home, a place that constitutes a spiritual or moral core, and in which *life* engages *things*.

Heidegger's text overflows with references to construction and architecture: the Heidelberg bridge, the German *Autobahn*, his own house in the Black Forest. In the same way, his reflections on the dwelling space lean in the direction of both the radical and the fundamental. Following from Husserl's critique of abstract Cartesian space, Heidegger links the essence of spatiality to the experience of the subject who is in the world. The space of dwelling is not a geometrical but an existential one, resulting from our phenomenological perception of place. Its construction is grounded in experience. As in so many of Heidegger's texts, this reflection on dwelling is an indictment of technical civilization and its loss of authenticity: it serves as an appeal to those who have the task in hand to think of the house as the response to the essential need for a rooted, constitutive dwelling, and a rejection of quantitative and inessential habitation. In contrast, Heidegger calls for a *qualitative* dwelling, one that would situate men between the earth and the gods.

The fact that similar aims were being formulated at the same time and in the same context of postwar destruction—both by those young architects committed to a revision of modernism's mechanized urban and architectural production and by a philosopher invited to reflect on the problem of dwelling in the contemporary world—manifestly reveals the correlation of their concerns, aspirations, and viewpoints.

Humanism

The ultimate referential grounding for the dominant system of values in the new European architectural scene of the fifties could be described by the term *humanism*. Clearly, this is a word that has been applied to a variety of historical situations, yet it nonetheless underwent a renewal of its synthesizing capacity within the existentialist climate in favor of the actual human subject, taking into account his or her actual experience, angst, and lived knowledge of specific space and time.

If it can be said that the key terms in the period between the wars were those referencing notions of progress, rationality, or happiness, then the postwar years can similarly be encapsulated by an ethical notion, according to which the personal universe of each individual—his or her intimate and subjective reality—serves as architecture and urbanism's principal goal. Josep Lluís Sert's recurring concern during this period, for example, was to arrive at a more human city; it was precisely this issue that provided the theme for CIAM VIII, which took place at Hoddesdon in 1951 and whose report was subtitled *Towards the Humanisation of Urban Life*. The key concept of the deliberations of these convened architects, supposedly representative of the most genuine modern tradition, was that of the core. The word's plurality of meanings perfectly exemplifies the type of concerns that guided the young revisionists in their opposition to the Athens Charter.

In effect, the core is at once the central nucleus of a thing, the center of a fruit, and the heart of a human being or some other living organism. The most innovative debate during this period about the core of the city as a new zone to be considered within the separate dispositions of the different urban functions thus involved not only establishing the need for a multiform and maximally social city center, but also, above all, characterizing this centrality as the heart of the city; in other words, as the physical locus traditionally regarded as the seat of the most elevated human emotions, those, for example, most necessary to the plenitude of an architecture in search of a new humanism.

The understanding of the core as a human heart emerged from an architectural debate in which function seemed to have yielded to passion. One can precisely chart this humanistic shift across the pages of the CIAM VIII collection, *The Heart of the City: Towards the Humanisation of Urban Life*, one of the most significant theoretical urban statements of this period.

When in 1959 Aldo van Eyck put forth his contribution to the ongoing reflection on the problems of architecture, he did so with the question "Is architecture going to reconcile basic values?" With his conviction that human nature embraces archaic principles that are at all times fundamentally the same, he positioned himself directly within the perspective of existential humanism. Quoting from Martin Buber, and against the background of his passionate interest in anthropology, van Eyck declared his commitment to ensuring that the new architecture should breathe—his own expression—in unison with human breathing.

Spain's José Antonio Coderch, briefly a member of Team X, similarly represents this prioritizing of the existentially spiritual that manifested itself in a rejection of all general theories and a call for a concrete, experiential approach to specific situations. Advocating a Christian humanism, Coderch added his voice to the chorus of appeals to the essential in man—thus gendered and singular—as the necessary corrective to the abstract, general, and mechanized points of view inherited from the avant-garde. This humanist program is neither accidental nor exclusively the domain of the architect. On the contrary, it is none other than the specific version by which this field of practical activity sought to respond to the calls to humanism then being issued by philosophers, artists, and intellectuals. This was a time when the work of a thinker such as Max Scheler—a disciple of Edmund Husserl and, as such, oriented along phenomenological lines—was widely read. Scheler's book *Man's Place in the Cosmos* was a bestseller during this period: it presented itself as an essay in philosophical anthropology, an attempt to explain not the general principles or categories of reality and thought but the personal, intimate experience of man within the infinity of the cosmos and historical time.

Jean-Paul Sartre contributed to the debate on humanism with his 1946 text "Existentialism Is a Humanism." Here existentialism—that is, Sartre's own philosophy—is presented as the abandonment of the entire metaphysical tradition in order to construct another kind of thinking based on the specific, lived reality of human beings. This widely propagated text prompted a response—oblique, as his replies were wont to be—from Martin Heidegger, in which, under the pretext of friendly correspondence with Jean Beaufret, Heidegger takes up the fluid category of humanism, as defined by Sartre, in order to carry it off into a problematic yet necessary zone. Heidegger's humanism resides in the method—phenomenological—and in the aim—the attempt to reconcile contemporary man with his technological world. But his is a humanism that requires assembly; more than a datum, it is an objective to be attained—problematic, and perhaps impossible.

The metaphors of the heart, the appeal to the human, and the growing awareness of anthropology are references that might serve as a guide to understanding the postwar phenomenon of architectural organicism. Mechanicism and organicism ask to be seen, within the intellectual tradition of twentieth-century architecture, as the opposition of two contrasting models, two metaphors by means of which architecture sought to find a formal model that would afford it an overall explication. Many historians of this period have spoken of a conflict between the mechanicists and organicists, as if this constituted some definitive or exclusive explanation. Indeed, it would seem to be possible to trace the genealogy of these two traditions, so that the mechanistic current ("constructivist," "Schlemmerian," "Picabian," "Corbusierian") could be situated in opposition to that other, organicist strand ("Wrightian," "Vandeveldian," "Scharounian," "Ernstian," "Aaltoian"). But such morphosymbolic oppositions lead nowhere. It would be far more useful to shift this potential duality, whose most polemical formulations were framed by Lewis Mumford, Richard Neutra, and Bruno Zevi, onto different ground: that of the association of organicism and humanism. "Organicism is a humanism" is an assertion that could have been made by either Alvar Aalto or Richard Neutra, for whom nature was not architecture but rather the model from which to produce an architecture in consonance with man, with the human scale.

In place of abstraction, architects committed to existential realism sought essential humanism within the realm of the vernacular, anterior to any cultural or technological contamination, as if those architectures without architects, so dear to Bernard Rudofsky, could form the basis of a tellurian force of nature from which our human substance emanates. This linking of organicism and humanism did not occur randomly but was a consequence of the crisis of rationalist architecture, of functionalism, and the new technology. Were Heidegger's problematic humanism to have taken material form, it might have been as this organic search for the lost human scale of buildings and cities.

The New Aesthetics

Existentialism, that child of phenomenology, engendered an innovative aesthetic system whose diffusion was to have a direct effect both on architecture and on the way that architecture was thought and explained throughout the crisis of the fifties.

Within the phenomenological tradition, the first datum is that of the intentionality of consciousness: that is to say, there is no system of objects governed by formal laws that might guarantee aesthetic efficacy. Instead, in the first instance, what exists is the subject's willingness to establish relations with a world that is to be constructed through the mediation of the body. The subject, who is a nothing, a useless passion, constructs the world by looking ahead, through openings, and through consciousness. The work of art is a gesture that emanates from the body. For Sartre or for Maurice Merleau-Ponty, what is produced is not the opening of the subject toward ideal values. Sartre's theory is that the intentionality of the subject is mundane, anchored in a world that is constructed on the basis of perception, imagination, and emotion. The other of the subject's body is presented as a production of the body itself. For Merleau-Ponty, the entire problem around which his fundamental philosophical writings revolve is that of breaking away from solipsism. In other words, the subject's body establishes the world on the basis of something that causes it to come out of itself. The idealist notions of concept, idea, spirit, and representation are substituted in Merleau-Ponty by those of articulation, edge, dimension, level, and configuration. Such empirical grounding ultimately provided the basis for Gestalt psychology, wherein evidence proceeds from the aesthetic-perceptual experience. Merleau-Ponty posited the issue in these terms from his earliest writings, those describing the nature and primacy of perception, through to his last, unfinished philosophical work on the visible and the invisible. He is the most systematic of the existentialists in the matter of laying down the bases of a non-normative process of being, from which we produce our relationship with the objects that make up our environment. Anyone familiar with the reflections of architects such as Ernesto Rogers or Paul Virilio will immediately ascertain the impact of these existentialists' phenomenological thinking on mid-twentieth-century architecture.

The crisis of values following World War II, which we are analyzing here, was responsible for the rejection of aesthetic systems based on the nineteenth-century idealist search for beauty. The visual was thus supplanted by total, synesthetic, productive perception. With the overthrow of general principles, the aesthetic was transformed from the imitation of a model to the subjective production of elementary perceptual experiences, capable of generating signification through emotion. The theoretical work of such writers as Rudolf Arnheim and Sven Hesselgren took as its starting point the phenomenology of perception, and consequently was liberated from all previously determined demands. The frontiers between the artistic and the emotive were thereby dissolved, freeing architecture from the constraints of having to produce certain effects or adapt to specific contents. Architecture, as well as every other field of aesthetic creation, acquired absolute freedom of perceptual experimentation, evidenced not only by the abandonment of certain codified stylemes of the modern tradition but in the opening toward highly experimental positions in the matter of forms, materials, and spaces.

The evident dismembering of the modern language that took place at this time finds its plausible explanation in the new aesthetic conception born of existential phenomenology. Colors, textures, lights, forms, spaces, not to mention a renascent decorativism and an opening up to the free play of experimentation, gave rise not only to brutalism but also to Neo-Liberty, to vernacularized organicism, and to the experimental hypertechnologism of Félix Candela, Pier Luigi Nervi, and R. Buckminster Fuller.

From the Individual to Society

The logical subsequent step was the critique of phenomenological individualism, and the move toward determining a more social logic as the basis of architectonic form. In Sartre and Merleau-Ponty, not in Heidegger or Karl Jaspers, and very much in Georg Lukács and Erich Fromm, the impact of Marxism was a decisive factor in directing this new shift toward the social. The critique of orthodox modernism made way in turn for a social critique of architecture. Ethical commitment in the terms of class struggle ushered in the first radical critiques of architecture. The Situationist International of Asger Jorn, Guy Debord, and Raoul Vaneigem sought to replace the internationalism of the last CIAMs and Team X with a more political and economic form of internationalism.

Consumption as the motor driving aesthetic production; the class ideology pervading all artistic production; the unviability of the modern city in its fostering of new problems of confrontation and social segregation; skepticism of the images of the collective unconscious inherited from surrealism and from a phenomenological reading of daily life: these critiques were to produce a new Bauhaus, an imaginist Bauhaus, in which the Situationists put on trial the new order that, on the basis of the miraculous economic milieu of the late fifties and early sixties, had been instituted in art, architecture, and the city.

Ethical humanism and aesthetic phenomenology enjoyed their moment of greatest influence on architecture during the fifties. Self-realization, experimental production, total aesthetic freedom, and the dissolution of the modern tradition as a rationally elaborated method, all served as points of support for innumerable works of architecture in which the individual experience, the primacy of the private, the antimonumental, and the incorporation of anthropologico-vernacular materials and techniques—the pursuit, in short, of a *degree zero* for architecture—constituted the common ground on which works and architects as apparently dissimilar as Aalto, Neutra, van Eyck, Rogers, Kahn, Nervi, and Fuller could come together.

Weak architecture evokes, from the outset, an allusion (not difficult to apprehend) to the terms *weak thought* and *weak ontology* that Gianni Vattimo and subsequently other Italian, as well as French and German, thinkers have put into circulation in recent years. It seems to me that what really lies behind *four* the propositions of weak philosophy is an interpretation of our contemporary culture's international, aesthetic situation. It is this subtext that leads to the question: What role is accorded to architecture in the aesthetic system of contemporary weak thought?

In a recent essay on the question of realism in modern architecture, Manfredo Tafuri posed the problem of interpreting what we commonly refer to as modern architecture, concluding that the contemporary experience, embracing all of twentieth-century architecture, can no longer be read in any linear form. On the contrary, it presents itself to us as a plural, multiform, complex experience in which it is legitimate to cut sectional trajectories that run not only from top to bottom, from beginning to end, but also transversely, obliquely, and diagonally. In some sense, it is only by way of approximations of this kind that the diverse, plural experience of twentieth-century architecture allows us to unstitch and unravel the intrinsic complexity of the modern experience itself.

And it is in this same sense that I propose the utility of the term *weak architecture*. I propose it as a diagonal cut, slanting, not exactly as a generational section but as an attempt to detect in apparently quite diverse situations a constant that seems to me to uniquely illuminate the present juncture. The interpretation of the crisis of the modern project can only be effected from what Nietzsche called "the death of God"; that is to say, from the disappearance of any kind of absolute reference that might in some way coordinate, or "close," the system of our knowledge and our values at the point at which we articulate these in a global vision of reality.

The crisis of the thought of the classical age, as Michel Foucault called it, is a crisis produced by this loss of a ground, together with the loss, in the field of art, of an artistic project, produced on the basis of a desire to represent. In *Les mots et les choses*, Foucault sets out to explain in painstaking detail how the system of representation belongs to the episteme of the classical age: mimesis presents a certain manner of articulating the world of the visual—and thus the world of architecture; in short, it effectively represents a vision of a closed and complete universe as a finished totality.

But the end of the classical age, which Friedrich Nietzsche announced as an end without return, was in reality the exhaustion of something that still inspires—at least to some degree—what we have come to refer to as the modern project. This end is an "illusion," but I wish to bring into play here the ambiguity of that term in Castilian, for it can also express a sense of wishful belief, *ilusión* as simultaneously hope and delusion. Illusion implies a process, and that this process is oriented toward a certain end. In this sense, the project of the Enlightenment, the basis of modernity, still participates in a secular theism, in the idea that it is possible to discover an absolute reality, within which art, science, and social and political praxis can be constructed on the basis of universal rationality. When this system enters into crisis (and it does enter into crisis, precisely as a result of the impossibility of establishing a universal system), we find ourselves faced with the *real* crisis of the modern project and the perplexing—we might say critical—situation of our contemporaneity.

Nietzsche again, in *Human, All Too Human*, speaks of the need for a grounding without ground. In the field of aesthetics, literary, pictorial, and architectonic experience can no longer be founded on the basis of a system: not on a closed, economical system such as that of the classical age; not even on the *ilusión* of a new system such as that which the pioneers of modern design sought to establish. On the contrary, contemporary architecture, in conjunction with the other arts, is confronted with the need to build on air, to build in the void. The proposals of contemporary art are to be constructed not on the basis of any immovable reference, but under the obligation to posit for every step both its goal and its grounding.

I want to emphasize the role assumed by the aesthetic in this situation of the crisis of contemporary culture. Indeed, as is acknowledged in Nietzsche, for example, and also in Martin Heidegger's appropriation of Nietzschean thought, the aesthetic constitutes a particularly significant reference for contemporary experience. In the system of the classical age, the aesthetic was very much a specific area, linked precisely to the practice of the concrete, far removed from any pretensions to the totality of an ontological system. In contemporary experience, the aesthetic has, above all, the value of a paradigm. It is precisely through the aesthetic that we recognize the model of our richest, most vivid, most "authentic" experiences in relation to a reality whose outlines are vague and blurred. If, as Heidegger warned in his meditation on technology, science ultimately becomes routine, it is not difficult to see why culture should have shifted the center of its interests toward those regions formerly regarded as manifestly peripheral. The most "full," the most "alive," that which is felt as being experience itself, that in which the perceiving subject and perceived reality are powerfully fused, is the work of art.

This is not to suggest that in the contemporary world, aesthetic experiences are at the center of the referential system. On the contrary, they continue to occupy a peripheral position; but this peripheral position possesses not a marginal but a paradigmatic value. Aesthetic experiences constitute, in some sense, the most solid, the strongest model of—paradoxically, indeed—a weak construction of the true or the real, and thus assume a privileged position within the system of references and values of contemporary culture.

(We might recall here, parenthetically, the fortunes of the artistic in contemporary mass society. The proliferation of museums, the magnification of the figure of the artist, the existence of a massive consumption of printed and televised artistic images, the widespread appetite for information about the arts, all reflect, of course, an increasingly leisured society, but also relate precisely to the fact that, faced with the tedium of everyday, real, lived experience, of the scientific illusion, of work and production, the world of art appears as a kind of last preserve of reality, where human beings can still find sustenance. Art is understood as being a space in which the fatigue of the contemporary subject can be salved away.)

But we must not forget that this contemporary aesthetic experience is not normative: it is not constituted as a system from which the organization of all of reality might be derived. On the contrary, the present-day artistic universe is perceived from experiences that are produced at discrete points, diverse, heterogeneous to the highest degree, and consequently our approximation to the aesthetic is produced in a weak, fragmentary, peripheral fashion, denying at every turn the possibility that it might ultimately be transformed definitively into a central experience.

The aestheticism of the late nineteenth century consisted precisely in the wishful hope of proposing the experience of art as the backbone of the experience of reality. But it was in this Promethean effort to appropriate to itself something that was fleeting, fugitive, always a little beyond our reach, that the articulating capacity of the aesthetic experience was diluted and that this experience now presents itself as fragmentary and marginal. It is only from this peripheral position that the aesthetic continues to exercise its seductive influence, its power to unveil, its capacity to imply rather than to constitute the intense apprehension of reality.

This referential framework, which has particularly close links with the thinking of the mature Heidegger, also helps to illuminate certain efforts at interpreting our contemporary architectural milieu. With the hopes of clarifying this position, I would like to compare the above exposition with other approaches to and interpretations of the present situation that seem to me to offer much less satisfactory responses to that situation. In the context of architectonic culture, and starting with the experience of crisis, the first responses—the responses we perceive throughout the course of the sixties—are above all fundamentalist in nature. For the phenomenon of fundamentalism is not to be found only in religion, reactionary politics, and certain specific sectors of society; there has also been a fundamentalism in the field of architectural theory and practice.

These fundamentalisms operate in two directions. On the one hand, there are those who, when confronted with the crisis, have called for order in the form of a return to the essentials of the modern experience. Certain theoretical discourses, sustained by leading academics at the influential Istituto Universitario di Architettura in Venice, as well as certain positions adopted by the New York Five group in the late 1960s, put forth the claim that only by going back to what was essential, germinal, and initial in the modern experience—Le Corbusier's *purisme*, in effect—was it possible to find the true path, picking up once again the thread of authentic experience. These voices called for an established line of orthodoxy and correctness to counter the diversion and diversification of the time. This was, in my opinion, a fundamentalist expression of the modern tradition. While it was understood by some as the recovery of the most pristine language of the avant-garde movements of the twenties, for others this experience served to take them further: they sought the lost tradition of the modern in still more primal origins, tracing the founding moments of modernity back to the primary forms of the Enlightenment.

The architecture of the Tendenza in Italy amounted to nothing less than a call to fundamentalism: an attempt at rereading the hardest, most programmatic, most radical architecture of the strictest exponents of rationalism of the interwar years, as well as of the architects of the Enlightenment. It was no accident that this situation saw the popularizing of the most laudatory images of the work of the most intensely Enlightened architects, in an effort to proclaim origins and a return to original purity. Certainly figures such as Aldo Rossi have taken it on themselves to deny the possibility of this undertaking. Rossi's work increasingly asks to be seen as a process that is above all self-critical. More and more, he demonstrates a progressive loss of confidence in that fundamentalism that was so decisive in his book *The Architecture of the City*, and that has nevertheless metamorphosed in his recent work into an intimate, private game.

Whether it be through such an enlightened fundamentalism or the fundamentalism of a Richard Meier, repeating over and over the linguistic tropes of twenties purism, these responses, for all their good intentions, amount to nothing more than pure historicism. With their fine words and noble aims, they constitute merely nostalgic attempts to return to supposedly authentic roots, whether in Le Corbusier's Villa Savoye, in Ludwig Hilberseimer's desolate apartment blocks, in Claude-Nicolas Ledoux's drawings, or in any other source of iconography taken for the wellsprings of the true tradition.

In opposition to this fundamentalist illusion, Kenneth Frampton has proposed in recent years a more dialectical and thus less monist, less self-enclosed approach. With his idea of critical regionalism, Frampton has put into circulation a term that I personally consider somewhat unfortunate, but one that has at least introduced a dualist vision into the interpretation of the contemporary situation. Frampton's proposal possesses two clearly differentiated faces. On the one hand there is the idea (in my view, the more attractive) of *resistance*. In this, he has kept faith with the teachings of the Frankfurt School and with his conviction that only by means of a critical attitude toward reality is it possible for contemporary architecture to maintain a rigorous and nonconformist position. It is an attitude capable of distinguishing itself from trivial culture, from the perverse operations of market forces, toward which the only valid response is resistance. But alongside this notion of resistance, the idea of *regionalism* seems a good deal more ingenuous. Frampton's concept, of course, refers to a reading of Heidegger, most directly to the philosopher's text "Bauen, Wohnen, Denken." But one must be cautious when one refers to Heidegger, and that caution is not fully visible in Frampton's articulation of regionalism. On the one hand, Heidegger's writing represents a profound diagnosis of the diseases of the modern world: isolation, provisionality, displacement, and failure. But on the other hand, we now know to what extent the former rector of Freiburg's university was associated with the burgeoning Nazism of the thirties, how much he sustained positions that directly opposed the development of technology, and how much he resisted the loss of traditional values, such as the vernacular, the anti-urban, and the archaic, that had historically formed the basis of a reactionary streak in modernism. When Frampton claims for the new vernacularism the resonances of a reappropriation of the sense of place, of light, of the tectonic, and of the tactile over the purely visual—the categories in terms of which he has characterized the new regionalism—he is undoubtedly engaged in a useful operation: that of understanding that a "system" as such is no longer possible, and that it is therefore necessary to understand architectonic reality from a polycentric strategy. Nevertheless, I believe it is naive to accept at the same time the viability of certain tectonic categories that can only be intelligible within the order of the old political urban culture of the classical age, a culture in which building, dwelling, and thinking constituted a unity. What in Heidegger is a tremulous verification of the disappearance of an already endangered world becomes, in Frampton and in other theoreticians of contemporary architecture, a phenomenologically ingenuous restoration that reveals little or no sense of the contemporary crisis.

Massimo Cacciari, in one of those brilliant and ferocious texts he so often produces, is withering in his dismissal of such excessively immediate interpretations of Heidegger's writings. For Heidegger, Cacciari claims, the metropolitan experience is constructed not through *dwelling* but through *desertion*: a desolation that in some sense constitutes the ground or root of the metropolitan condition. Turning to a late text by Heidegger, Cacciari suggests that, in point of fact, the contemporary metropolitan experience is not one that allows us to speak of dwelling in the same terms as a citizen of Periclean Athens or the Rome of Sixtus V; unlike theirs, our metropolitan dwelling is split, diversified, subject to absence more than to presence. Poetry, that is to say what is vitalizing and grounding, does not construct the entirety of our daily surroundings but is simply the experience of absence. It is the experience of absence, in other words, that draws the contours of the metropolitan subject. If Frampton's proposals are of interest only to the extent that they have expanded the vision of reality and introduced the need to accept as incontrovertible the diversity of modern experiences, Cacciari's critique, underlining as it does the sense of absence, brings us to a concept of central importance in contemporary criticism—a concept that directly stems from this experience of the fragmentary: the archaeological.

The specific use of the term *archaeology* derives from French poststructuralism, primarily from the writings of Foucault, and has been taken up by thinkers such as Jacques Derrida and applied to the analysis of literary communication as a process of deconstruction. But this notion of archaeology comes into its own as a tool for describing, in almost physical fashion, the superimposed reading(s) of tectonic reality: of a reality that can no longer be regarded as a unitary whole but appears instead as the overlapping of different layers. Faced with this reality, the work of art can do no more than reread or redistribute this system of superimpositions. The notion of archaeology evidently introduces the idea that what confronts us is not a reality that forms a closed sphere but a system of interweaving languages. Nobody could be so naive as to imagine that, for archaeology, the system of knowledge of the past can be constituted by a simple accumulation of the objects uncovered by excavation. Rather, these objects present themselves as the outcome of a process of decomposition of superimposed systems, systems that nowhere touch, systems that move independently according to their own logic. Language, too, is a diversity that can no longer be read in a linear fashion. We can no longer believe that the reality of a signified responds to the precision of a signifier, as Derrida would say. Instead, it forms a magma that is at once producer and produced. Only a task of deconstruction, a work of analysis and comprehension of the processes of juxtaposition, is capable of elucidating certain relationships.

There is no doubt that this way of thinking has a very direct translation in the experience of the production of form, and thus, by inclusion, of architectonic form. In effect, the experience of certain recent architectures is the experience of superimposition. The signified is not constructed by means of an order but by means of pieces that may ultimately touch; that approach one another, at times without touching; that draw nearer to one another yet never make contact; that overlap, that offer themselves in a discontinuity in time whose reading as juxtaposition is the closest approximation to reality at our disposal.

At the same time, the relationship between archaeology and language has introduced a fundamental innovation into the discourse of contemporaneity: the centrality of the notion of time. This is, expressly, a time different from the time of the classical age. Contemporary time—today's fragmented reality of overlapping virtual and "real" times that was artistically anticipated in the writings of James Joyce, Robert Musil, and Mario Vargas Llosa—is presented precisely as juxtaposition: a discontinuity; something that is in complete contrast to a single, unique, closed and complete system. Time in the architecture of the classical age could be reduced simply to zero (as in the experience of Renaissance centrality) or at most constitute a controlled time—a time with a beginning and an orderly and ordered expansion (which was entirely the experience of baroque temporality). In fact, it is not by chance that Giedion's presentation of modern time in *Space, Time and Architecture* begins by analyzing baroque architecture. In some sense, that means that for the first generation of modern architects, time/space was defined as a continuity more than as a fragment or juxtaposition, as it had already been anticipated and explored in literature, theater, music, and other disciplines.

Contemporary time, however, cannot sustain these classical or baroque illusions. It presents itself as a diffracted explosion in which there is no unique and single time from which we can construct experience. There are, instead, *times*, various times, the times with which our experience of reality produces itself. The confrontation with and the attempt to understand this problem of the diversity of times embraces the whole struggle of art in the twentieth century. Time in the cubist experience, futurist time, time in Dadaism, time in the formalist experiences of the optical and the Gestalt experiences of formalism, are versions of a diversified, juxtaposed time that constitutes one of the basic conditions of modernity. It is nevertheless clear that this condition was not always fully understood by the masters of modern architecture, who in many cases thought that what was needed was a time divorced from the centralism of perspectival vision, but which might perfectly well be a time organized from the linear viewpoint, after the fashion of the cinematographic sequence. In Le Corbusier, the *promenade architecturale* is not a diversity but an itinerary that admits the possibility of control. This is the illusory hope that we find not only in Le Corbusier but equally in Giedion and in other foundational architectures and histories of the modern experience. What is abundantly clear is that, increasingly, metropolitan culture offers us times as diversity, and the recognition of this is something that an archaeological approach to the languages of architecture has manifested in a number of ways.

This diversity of times becomes absolutely central in what I have chosen to call weak architecture. In sympathy with the visions of Joyce and others, and in contrast to the idealist narrative sustained by Giedion, these architectures transform the aesthetic experience of the artwork, and specifically of architecture, into *event*. Temporality does not present itself as a system but as an aleatory instant that, responding above all to chance, is produced in an unforeseeable place and moment. In certain works of contemporary art, in dance, in music, in installation, the experience of the temporal as event, occurring once and then gone forever, ably explicates a notion of temporality that finds in the event its fullest form of expression.

If the notion of event allows us to approximate more closely one of the characteristics of weak architecture, the Deleuzean notion of the *pli*, or fold, is no less definitive. Gilles Deleuze published a book that, under the apparently innocuous guise of a summary of Foucault's thought, set out to develop a whole project constitutive of a contemporary vision of reality. The seductive appeal of this text lies, among other things, in its grasp of the fact that in contemporary thought the objective and the subjective are not different and opposing fields but constitute what he calls "folds of a single reality." For architecture, this notion of the fold proves exceptionally illuminating. Reality emerges as a continuum in which the time of the subject and the time of external objects go round together on the same looped tape, with the encounter of objective and subjective only occurring when this continuous reality folds over in a disruption of its own continuity.

Eugenio Trias, in his book *Los límites del mundo*, speaks of the untimely nature of the contemporary situation and contemporary art; untimely in the sense of sudden, unanticipated coagulations of reality, events that are produced not through linear and foreseeable organization but through folds and fissures, as Foucault himself sometimes says, that in some way afford the refuge, the tremulous fluttering of a brief moment of poetic and creative intensity.

Together with the precarious nature of the event and this untimely fold of reality, what I have called weak architecture is always decorative. Let no one be shocked: decoration is a *parole maudite*, a dirty word in the modern tradition, yet there is nonetheless a clear need to go back and reflect on the significance of the term and on the fundamental meaning of the notion of decorum that underlies that of decoration. I am aware of the decisive signification that this term exercises in, for example, the thinking of Leon Battista Alberti and in humanist aesthetics generally. Here, however, I mean to propose a different use of the word. As it is most commonly employed, in the sense it has in the decoration magazines, in its everyday use, the decorative is the inessential; it is that which presents itself not as substance but as accident: something complementary that will even lend itself, in Walter Benjamin's terms, to a reading that is not attentive but distracted, and which thus offers itself to us as something that enhances and embellishes reality, making it more tolerable, without presuming to impose itself, to be central, to claim for itself that deference demanded by totality. Decoration, then, or the decorative condition of contemporary art and architecture, not in the sense of vulgarity, of triviality, of the repetition of established stereotypes, but as a discreet folding back to a perhaps secondary function, a pulling back to a function that projects beyond the hypothetical ground of things. The text in which Heidegger deals with the question of sculpture in space, *Die Kunst und der Raum*—a text based on a conversation with Eduardo Chillida, and in fact published with a series of beautiful etchings by the Basque sculptor— addresses precisely this question: that the decorative is not of necessity a condition of trivialization of the vulgar, but simply constitutes a recognition of the fact that for the work of art—sculptural or architectonic—an acceptance of a certain weakness, and thus of relegation to a secondary position, may possibly be the condition of its greatest elegance and, ultimately, its greatest significance and import.

In conclusion, I would like to gloss one last characteristic of weak architecture: monumentality. We must resort once again here to wordplay. This is not a question of monumentality as representation of the absolute. The monument in the classical age is the center, it is the *imago Dei*, the figuration of a transcendent divinity that guarantees the consistency of time. The figure of the king in the middle of the Royal Square thus constitutes the emblem of the power that hierarchically orders a given public space. The obelisk at the central point of the perspective is the monument that guarantees the coherence and immovability of the representational visual structure. It is not about this monument that I wish to speak, because quite clearly this is the monument that has provoked the crisis in the contemporary situation. The monumentality of weak architecture is not continuous with the monuments of the classical age in either geometric or ideological value, but only in what remains within the present context of that condition of the root term *monitu*; that is to say, of recollection.

Heidegger, once again, in *Die Kunst und der Raum*, quotes some words of Goethe that I would like to repeat here: "It is not necessary for the true always to take on material form, it is enough that it should flutter to and fro, like a spirit, promoting a kind of accord; as when the companionable pealing of a bell rings out, bringing us some little measure of peace." The idea of monument that I want to bring in here is that which we might find in an architectonic object: for all its being an opening, a window on a more intense reality, at the same time its representation is produced as a vestige, as the tremulous clangor of the bell that reverberates after it has ceased to ring; as that which is constituted as pure residuum, as recollection. In his *Architecture of the City*, Aldo Rossi employed the term monument to signify permanence, because he was then still operating within a monistic conception of reality and a fixed and static definition of the city. In contrast, the notion of monument I have sought to put forward here is bound up with the lingering resonance of poetry after it has been heard, with the recollection of architecture after it has been seen.

This is the strength of weakness; that strength which art and architecture are capable of producing precisely when they adopt a posture that is not aggressive and dominating, but tangential and weak.

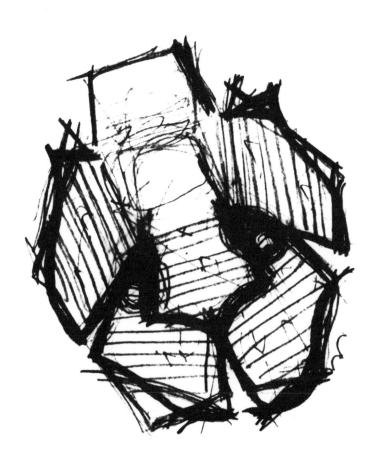

Autonomy
The avant-garde's assumptions about history, time, change, and social relations were subjected to a radical critique during the 1960s. Symbolized by the images of 1968, this critique consisted of a broad series of attacks on the teleological and progressive model that had *five* invested works of art and architecture with meaning. This model was swept away in a whirlwind: youthful and utopian, yet at the same time pessimistic and self-critical.

The revolutionary situation of '68 lent support to new, more limited and cautious propositions, and eventually resulted in our present panorama of incertitude and desolation. From pessimism provoked by Soviet tanks in Prague and young Americans fighting pointlessly in Vietnam we have moved to the obscenity of the high-tech bombing of Baghdad and the stupor induced by images of Kurds fleeing from their own country.

Within academia, the linear conception of history as the limitless progress of humanity was shattered during the sixties by structuralist thinking. More than a philosophy, structuralism presented itself as a method. A tool for explaining reality, born of the formalist linguistics of the Prague circle, structuralism extended easily into the cultural fields of anthropology, the social sciences, law, literature, and art. On the basis of analogies with verbal language, structuralism went on to dissect parallel processes in any field of reality whatsoever.

This diffusion of the linguistic paradigm had two immediate consequences. The first consisted of understanding any cultural product or process as a language in itself, and as such subject to the interdependence of signifier and signified. And given that everything was language, everything was also a process of signification: in short, everything was communication. Art, social conduct, the economic mechanisms of production and consumption, and architecture were all channels of communication, *mass media* through which specific messages were transmitted according to, as Marshall McLuhan claimed, the characteristics of the medium.

The structuralist vision of culture and society evolved into pansemiology and the mediatic conception of reality. Umberto Eco, Jean Baudrillard, and Roland Barthes spread the good news of structuralism as communication. But this thinking, understood as a neutral scientific method, as a simple objectivist derivation from Husserlian phenomenology, had another fundamental feature: structures, languages, and processes of signification were, by definition, autonomous, closed, purely and exclusively devoted to their own self-sustenance. Structuralist analysis reveals the self-regulatory mechanisms at work within the totalities of relations of production or architectonic repertoires. Its fundamental methodological principle is that once a structural system has been identified, what should then be examined is its internal mechanism, the protocols governing the economy of its movements, and, finally, the system's potential to deploy itself.

The emergence of structuralism had fundamental consequences upon the field of artistic production. When Joseph Kosuth wrote in 1969, "Art indeed exists for its own sake," he was formulating the principle of art's autonomy. The rediscovery of Marcel Duchamp by conceptual artists signified, on the one hand, the disappearance of all reference to anything beyond the universe of artistic products itself and, on the other, the prioritization of the communicative-linguistic orientation in the understanding of artistic activity.

The conceptual artist puts the idea before the materiality of the object. Exposing the logical procedures by which ideas are transmitted in artistic communication is the primary aim of the conceptualists' aesthetic program. In the work of Dennis Oppenheim, Robert Morris, Jan Dibbets, Bruce Nauman, Edward Ruscha, and Kosuth, it is not the political, ecological, or formal message that is interesting. What feeds this work is the artists' self-interrogating reflection on their activity as producers of art and on the work's self-referentiality. "Art is a proposition about art, presented in the context of art as a commentary on art," wrote Kosuth, hammering home the autonomy of procedures, contents, and references intrinsic to artistic production. There is no tautology in this assertion, just as there is no tautology in the proposition, "Art as idea as idea," which has become the key leitmotif of today's artists.

Even more. Art is not the object: it cannot be identified with an artifact that we appropriate independently of the process by means of which it was conceived and realized. The process is more important than the work of art. More important than the finished, isolated object are the ideas that made it possible. Artistic communication is produced at the moment we are able to understand the object as the result of a structure, as an always provisional state that proceeds from prior studies and that will make subsequent development possible. Only from the structure of the complex whole and the successive systems of signifiers and signifieds are we given the possibility of receiving the idea, of participating in the self-referential and autonomous messages of the processes of artistic production.

In architecture too since the mid-1960s we find a manner of understanding objectives parallel to those just described in the plastic arts. In *L'architettura della città* of 1966, Aldo Rossi critiqued the functionalist tradition, the dependence of architectonic form on something beyond its own logic and the internal processes of its transformation. For Rossi, "the explanation of urban facts in terms of their function must be rejected when it seeks to illustrate their constitution and form. Such an explanation is repressive rather than enlightening because it inhibits the study of forms and a knowledge of the world of architecture according to its own authentic laws." The call for an autonomous understanding of architecture based on the body of theory intrinsic to it—set forth in treatises and manuals—and the definition of morphological and typological data as essential references in the analysis of works of architecture and urban design reveal the influence of structuralist thinking upon the domain of architecture.

Not only do his references to Claude Lévi-Strauss and Roman Jakobson clearly indicate the nature of the support underpinning Rossi's theories; his actual practice as an architect also reveals his true interests. Over the years[*] Rossi's work has articulated a discourse from the *interior* of architecture, whereby the interrelation of the main typologies or the play of a figuration reduced to its essential qualities constitute the process of architectural production. An architecture that neither starts nor finishes with the object, Rossi's production shows itself to be an endless structural interplay between types and images in constant interaction, such that the presentation of the idea, as a play of figures, constitutes the fundamental aim of his work.

The sense of disillusion experienced by many upon seeing a Rossi building constructed on an actual site and from concrete materials derives from the fact that the building thus asks to be considered objectively or functionally, while its author tries to call attention instead to the process revealed in his drawings, so that the construction of the building is an episode in an architectonic discourse understood as autonomous and thus indifferent to construction or use.

When Arthur Drexler, Colin Rowe, and Kenneth Frampton identified certain shared features in the work of five New York architects in the exhibition and catalogue entitled *Five Architects* in 1971, they advocated the autonomy of the discipline and its exclusive dependence on essential figures. The internal history of modern architecture has placed this play of repertoires within the hands of certain architects concerned purely with syntax: for these architects, semantics constitute not so much a goal to be reached as a point from which to depart. The idea, defined by sketches, not by built work, overtakes the importance of the "real thing." It is not only Rowe's remarks on the failure of modern architecture that are highly significant, but also his insistence that it is the *idea* that draws together a number of architects previously and subsequently as dissimilar as the five featured in the exhibition.

Autonomy once more. An interior game within the field of action established by modern architecture in the first moments of its existence. No matter that this very autonomy was subsequently dispersed along different paths: toward experimentation with new semantic repertoires in the case of Michael Graves; toward investigation of syntax in Peter Eisenman's work of the 1970s; and in search of the primal myth and founding event in the work of John Hejduk. In all of these, architecture was a universe sufficient unto itself, nourished on its own history and emerging from the interior of its own rules and protocols just as Minerva, recreating the myth of the hermaphrodite in the elegance of the classical world, was born from Jupiter's head.

Radical Critique

The structuralist project was simply one aspect of a much more radical critique of culture and art. The Frankfurt School had already formulated the lines of a limitless self-criticism. The wounds inflicted by World War II—destruction and holocaust—scarred into a total mistrust of the cultural values of the so-called western world. If existentialism constituted a subjective and individual response, the critical theory of the Frankfurt group sought to offer an objective solution. The cultural program elaborated by Theodor Adorno and Max Horkheimer and the hyper-criticism of Herbert Marcuse and Jürgen Habermas traced an intellectual approach seeking not new proposals but honest intellectual action in all artistic and philosophical production.

The special attention that critical theory accords to the field of aesthetic production makes it particularly important for our analysis. There cannot be a progressive art, or a progressive literature, or a progressive architecture. All is mystification, in the Marxist sense of the term, that is, all is ideology. The message of the artistic production of modernity is mystifying, enshrining the trickery that emanates from an alienated society and proposing the values of a single class, which embody party interests and reflect the unresolved social contradiction present in what Adorno liked to call *Spätkapitalismus*, or late capitalism. The only function for the intelligentsia is to act critically: there is no longer any attempt to propose new programs; no space from which to define the future. Karl Mannheim set limits to utopian thought in resuming, as the members of the Frankfurt School had done, the Marxist critique of utopian socialism and ideology. Critical theory provoked a reaction within the field of artistic production and self-reflection, turning it in the direction of nihilism, in the sense of discrediting any kind of productive activity. Artistic practice was supplanted by theoretical practice, to use Louis Althusser's felicitous expression. All production is ideology, a consequence of the dominant forces in the economic structure, and it is all based on class struggle. Art and architecture are only superstructural reflections of this ideological hegemony.

In the face of such evidence, artistic production had to be replaced by critical action. The work of the operatives producing art could not consist of simply accumulating ideological products, but rather had to develop a critique of the ideologies underlying all artistic discourse. The Hegelian discourse on the death of art was reborn. What had been conventionally considered as artistic production was transformed into action: critical, unmasking, destructive.

The production of groups such as Cobra, Fluxus, and the later neo-Dadaism of happenings and anti-art events should be understood as the expression, within artistic practice itself, of artists' mistrust of their medium for anything other than its own destruction. The adoption of the forms of everyday life in order to disrupt them aggressively was the habitual method of Allan Kaprow, Wolf Wostell,

Al Hansen, and Hermann Nitsch, but also, at times, of Yoko Ono, Joseph Beuys, Claes Oldenburg, Walter De Maria, and others.

The smashing of automobiles or TV sets; the showering of blood and strewing of viscera across the immaculate space of a theater or art gallery; the piling up of coarse flabby nudes; the combination of electronic music, splashes of paint, mechanical noise, photographically produced optical deformations: all of these acts of vandalism, annihilation, extermination, and ruin constitute the artistic translation of the critical program. The death of art announced by philosophy becomes visible in this aggressive and brutal recovery of Dadaist strategies generated above all by way of the ever greater mythification of Marcel Duchamp and Walter Benjamin: Duchamp as the producer of objects that confront the conventions of art with sarcasm, in opposition to their retinal value, their unrepeatability; Benjamin as the heterodox thinker, outside the academy, assembling an uncompletable discourse of fragments, prophet of the downfall of the capitalist world, bitterly evoking the past.

Guy Debord and Raoul Vaneigem's Situationism also developed under these conditions of radical critique as theoretical practice. The Situationists revealed modern urban planning's relationship to the psychopathology of everyday life: the dictatorship of rational design principles born of a determinist, para-fascist Bauhaus; an incipient ecological critique; the vulgarization of erotic myths disseminated by means of advertising images; the experience of urban space not as the result of a compositional order but as a *dérive*, an erratic accumulation of synesthetic experiences. Predominant in all of these propositions is the critique of contemporary culture. Not the grand, high, official culture of museums, concerts, literature, and art, but mass culture, the culture of everyday life produced by the powerful media of advertising, television, comics, architecture, and urban design. Yet another consequence of the critical theory of the Frankfurt School was the radicalism of the architectural historians and critics of Venice's Istituto Universitario di Architettura, Manfredo Tafuri, with the intellectual support first of Asor Rosa, Mario Tronti, and Antonio Negri, and of Massimo Cacciari and Franco Rella in the 1980s, was the spokesperson for a radical critique of modern architecture. *Per una critica dell'ideologia architettonica*, first published in 1969 and later reworked in the brief *Progetto e utopia* of 1973, is the most significant manifesto of global criticism of the modern production of architecture as ideology in the negative Marxist sense of the term, and in the more precise definition accorded it by the thinking of the Frankfurt School. Ultimately, it is the global critique of modern art as formulated by Georg Lukács in his extensive body of theoretical, and more especially aesthetic, work that interests Tafuri, as does the connection between the critique of architecture and the critique of society on which he founds his discourse. The exposure of the ideological, which is to say mystifying, condition of modern architectonic language is a thoroughly political act. It is a call for the destruction of architecture. For this reason, the historical justification structured by Tafuri, from Brunelleschi to the present, is presented as a history of mystification and deceit. It is the recidivist mechanism by means of which, beneath the grand emancipating aims of architectural and urban design proposals, ruin, desolation and nothingness always appear.

It would be impossible to trace the course of contemporary architecture without offering a privileged place to negativism and radical criticism, both within the general framework of aesthetic theory and in its particular translation into the contexts of the figurative arts and architecture.

The radical critique of architectural ideology, rooted in that first, powerful formulation in Venice, is visible in Europe and the United States in the troubled consciences of those architects engaged in the professional practice of architecture, and in the aggressive confrontation between them and the producers of theoretical and critical discourse. This critique emerges in the tendentious reconstruction of modern history, as well as in the production of critical projects, projects posited as pure speculation on paper, whose purpose is nothing other than to demonstrate the impossibility of architecture. In the drawings of John Hejduk, Massimo Scolari, the members of Superstudio, and early Hans Hollein or Bernard Tschumi, the evocation of impossible architectures, of ruins, of spatial absurdities and of conceptual paradoxes is part of the same radical climate, sharing that same loss of confidence in the possibility of a truly buildable and culturally valid architecture.

Liberalism

At critical radicalism's opposite pole lie options whose origins must be sought in a liberal culture. The term *liberal* does not carry the same signification in the English-speaking countries as it does in Latin culture. For the former, *liberal* refers to a more or less open, progressive political posture, perhaps on occasion accompanied by a degree of radicalism; for the latter, *liberal* corresponds more strictly to the continuing influence of the political doctrines of nineteenth-century liberalism: the precedence of the individual over the collective; ideological tolerance, tinged with a fairly strong dose of subjectivism; pragmatic realism as opposed to the great totalitarian constructs of socialism or the old pre-democratic regimes. In Latin political terminology the word *liberal* applies to philosophical positions marked by a certain empirical realism and enlightened approach with regard to principles, societies, and political positions—the heir, in other words, of the democratic ideals of the social reformers who preceded the French Revolution, unwavering defenders of private property and the democratic organization of society. It is in this latter sense, then, that it is possible to speak of a cultural neoliberalism in apparently disparate positions within artistic and architectural creation.

The philosophical referents of this liberalism lie in British empiricism and more specifically in those thinkers for whom the study of logic and the philosophy of language were the foundation for every other consideration. Bertrand Russell, Karl Popper, A. J. Ayer, and even Ludwig Wittgenstein, to name some of the most significant figures of contemporary thought, were rigorous analysts of the limits of truth, both in the language of science and in languages organizing the conduct of ethics and feelings. Their repudiation of the metaphysical tradition and the Hegelian construction of history led them to reject historical method as a means of determining laws to govern the present. Their methodological caution in the human and social sciences led them to base statements on quantifiable proof of facts rather than on grand general claims. In principle, then, we find in aesthetic liberalism little sympathy for avant-garde art or the more daring proposals of experimental groups.

Ernst Gombrich and Colin Rowe, both closely linked to the great intellectual tradition of the Warburg Institute, and Ortega y Gasset, George Santayana, Isaiah Berlin, and T. S. Eliot: these are the names that are frequently referenced in liberal aesthetic discourse—a discourse that, in the 1970s and even the 1980s, enjoyed renewed vigor thanks to the crisis of the modern project. Structuralist autonomy and radical criticism have existed alongside the civilized realism of liberals who, while manifesting a certain tolerance, have championed a new representational realism in the domains of art and architecture. It is only in terms of these postulates that the recent hyperrealist tendency in the plastic arts becomes a comprehensible alternative to both abstraction and expressionism. The exhibition entitled "Réalismes," organized by the Pompidou Center in Paris in 1980, constituted the recovery of the academic figurative tradition, precursor to the analytical tradition of impressionism and kept alive by twentieth-century artists who positioned themselves well to one side of the avant-garde.

This realism has precise theoretical foundations. The relationship between subject and object is clear and stable and proceeds by means of imitation. Pictorial and sculptural realism entertains no doubts about reality and the truth of our perception of it. Its representation results from the attentive observation of reality and its orderly imitation in the volume of a bronze or on the surface of a canvas. In architecture, too, liberal realism achieved its most noted successes by way of two apparently divergent orientations united by a shared conception of knowledge and representation. The reappropriation of the repertoires of historical architecture by so-called postmodernist architects and the truth claim promulgated by high tech architects share a common confidence in the communication between the human subject and reality.

In the case of postmodern architecture, the realist procedure is evident in the following ways. The apparent historicism of reusing stylistic clichés from the past reveals full confidence in the possibility of repeating them for the future—the liberalism of Francis Fukuyama's *End of History*—and demonstrates faith in the communicative consistency of signs. From Robert Venturi and Philip Johnson to Robert Krier and Ricardo Bofill, the liberal cast of their ethical stance is perfectly in tune with their confidence about veraciously manipulating the signs of the architecture of other epochs.

The theoretical discourse of a Venturi or a Colin Rowe rests, for complexity or for collage, as much on the solidity of established codes as on their coexistence in a world of social communication in which no one can claim exclusive rights to a given language. Out of their tolerance, with their sense of the efficacy of the political economy of the great majority, they accept and promote a discursive system that is rich, various, and multiple, but ultimately transparent, decodable, transmissible, and truthful.

The architects of high tech are likewise liberals, convinced of the clear and definable correspondence between form and function, between the demands of construction and their technical resolution. The work of Norman Foster, Renzo Piano, Paul Virilio, and David Chipperfield corresponds to the ideal of the communication of the immaterial detected by Jean-François Lyotard in his reflections on communication in contemporary culture.

An ideal, resolute and sure, of the real possibility of quantitatively controlling the requirements of an architectonic program so as to provide it with an elegant and economic response lies at the base of an architecture that assumes the false modesty of being simply the appropriate technical answer to the well-defined requirements. Technical confidence, realism in the figuration of this clean relationship between form and function, tension and rigor, but also sureness and confidence, are the content of an architecture that is as well received by the technocrats as it is by those who ward off the constant dread of the technological menace.

An Untimely Art

The crisis of modernism referred to by the nihilists and fraudulently transcended by the cultivators of the images of communications and technology cannot be resolved within the self-absorption and self-reflection of structuralism. Poststructuralist thought has begun the task of thinking the world from the absence of foundation and the decomposition of historical time. Thinkers such as Gilles Deleuze have demonstrated the nonexistence of a platform from which it is possible to construct a vision of the world. There is no such platform, but rather *mille plateaux* (a thousand plateaus), a limitless multiplicity of positions from which it is possible only to erect provisional constructions. Nor is the reality of things and events organized along some continuous thread extended in the orderly succession of time. What we do today does not derive substance from reference to past experience, nor do we have the authority necessary to justify what we produce now in relation to what is to come. The notion of *le pli*, the fold, as glossed by Deleuze himself, supposes that space in this poststructural situation is made up of platforms, fissures, folds, infills, surfaces, and depths that completely dislocate our spatial experience. Our experience of time is also one of discrete occurrences. Out of the pain of feeling that we merely create instantaneous interpretations, we now find provisional significances. Ours is not a present in continuum between past and future, as claimed by the optimistic humanists of the Enlightenment. This is an untimely present, temporality lacking justification, and for that reason gratuitous and without finality.

This recent situation reinforces the Kantian notion that the aim of the aesthetic act is the production of objects whose end is exhausted in the act of production, converting them into ends without end. The hermeneutic thought

of Hans-Georg Gadamer or Hans Jauss proposes, as the key to understanding the significance of a work of art, the experience of its reception. In place of knowing the structures of artistic production, they appeal to the interchangeability of the interpretations produced by those who experience the work of art. This is certainly a Copernican twist in the way that it relativizes, or even makes parenthetical, the source from which the aesthetic object springs, concerning itself only with the vessels in which it is received and appropriated by hermeneutic processes of decoding. Deconstruction would thus be no more than the technology and the result of this hermeneutic reception, eliminating the author in order to give pride of place to the receivers. This position lacks legitimacy, however, inasmuch as it fails to reveal how reception takes place and how, ultimately, these texts, considered to be floating, rootless objects outside of space and time, are appropriated.

The experience of minimal art since the 1960s, and its less rigorous, more communicative European version, *arte povera*, introduces us to artistic experimentation reduced to the lower limit of the production of meaning in the work of art. We are not dealing here with the problem of expression as posed by expressionist subjectivism or the pathetic isolation of existentialism. Minimalism engages the activity of production, drawing on the elementary data of the external world. The minimalist vision, as Rosalind Krauss notes, is phenomenological rather than metaphysical. It proceeds not from the idea but from the experience. An installation, a spatial proposal by Donald Judd, Richard Serra, Robert Morris, or Richard Artschwager, is a return to a synesthetic perceptual moment prior to the retinal distinction of the plastic arts, yet there is no attempt to establish permanent typologies, or to evoke recognizable deep structures in the interpretation of the artistic object.

It is the provisional instant. The intransitive event. The proposition elevated into a place. The indefiniteness of the urban and metropolitan condition of minimalism's products is highly significant: it demonstrates the impossibility of trapping them in any planned, organized conception of urban space or structure. They erupt in untimely fashion. They are gratuitous. The end of these artifacts lies in the rejection of functional, linguistic, or mimetic justifications they establish.

There is also an untimely architecture born out of time without regard to any system of principles, traditions, or linguistic codes. It is that which, for good reason, presents a radical desolation, a groundlessness emerging out of the singularity of an event. I have drawn attention elsewhere to the *weakness* of architecture, a weakness having nothing to do with a lack of ability to manifest the conditions of the contemporary world and contemporary culture. Quite the contrary. This weakness is precisely the architectonic manifestation of the condition of contemporary culture. I would like to focus, for a moment, on the work of three present-day architects: Alvaro Siza, Tadao Ando, and Frank Gehry. I believe we find in all three the full and eloquent resonance of the condition of contemporary culture.

Just as in minimalism, the syntax with which the elements of construction are laid out in space in Siza's work is both abstract and temporary. There is no attempt to establish a procedure or to elaborate the architecture as the deconstruction of some previously existing architectonic text. The geometric dislocations, the slippings, the distortions of perpendicularity, and the incomplete anchoring of Siza's forms are the expression of an architecture produced *ex novo* every time. What provokes admiration or surprise in the work of the Portuguese architect is this provisional, novel quality of each project. The subtle lightness of his intentions and the reduction to the minimum of the semantic resources privilege all of the syntactic content. In a wholly different register, Ando's work also reveals this untimely condition. The interplay of the concrete volumes and the gridlike control of the dimensions of his buildings have nothing in common either with the remains of the universal metaphysics of the elements, as occurs in Louis Kahn, or with a supposed *mathesis universalis* descended from the modular architectures of Le Corbusier. In Ando, the production is unique to every scheme. Each is an independent experiment, perfectly separable from the others. These are largely self-defining designs. They obey no context. They do not imitate tradition. If they refer to the local culture, they do so as absence, as void, as the cancellation of every affirmation. They are artifacts that we must experience psychosomatically in their reality. They are not served up to us through representation, or even through visual appearance. The event occurs at a point, in an instant. There is no sense in explaining them in terms of the before or the after.

Although Gehry's architecture stems from a different approach, it too carries an untimely or inconclusive message. He proceeds like a plastic artist, especially in his method of configuration. There is no sense in talking of perversion or excess. Gehry's work is what it is, and his schemes make no reference to other schemes—different, earlier, or comparable. This is "installation" architecture, down to the deliberate fragility of its materials and deliberate carelessness with which it treats the tectonic, in the total absence of the Vitruvian *firmitas*. His projects originate in abstract forms. They are opaque to the expression of necessities, just as they tell us nothing about the architect's personality. They are at the opposite pole from any kind of contextual or autobiographical architecture. They erupt at some moment or other, always untimely, always unexpectedly. Each scheme is exhausted in itself, completely on the outside of any normative intention. They do not offer us any method. They do not affirm any absolute truth.

Deleuze, in his *Logique du sens* of 1969, contrasted the work of Chronos, the god of time, with that of Aeon, the divinity rescued by the Stoic philosophy of Marcus Aurelius. Chronos is the corporeal present. He measures the actions of bodies and binds past, present, and future together. Chronos is regulated, cosmic, infinite movement, guaranteed in the last analysis by Zeus, the father of the gods. He is time in all its fullness. For Aeon, by contrast, time is only the instant, without depth or extension. With him, everything rises to the surface and becomes instantaneous event. He has no need of the guarantees of gods. He is volatile and provisional. He has fled before we can catch him. As Plato says, he is atopical, without place. He is the "without cause," the random. Language does not come to him; it unfolds in him. Its meaning is unpredictable. Aeon's experience cannot be encoded or encapsulated. It erupts, untimely. Like the tale told by the actor on the stage, like the unexpected pirouettes of a graceful ballerina.

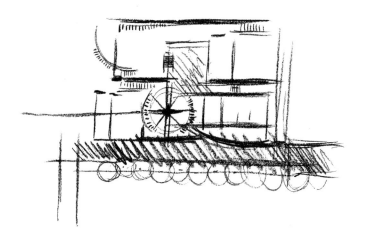

The belief that space
is a category proper
to architecture is a
modern notion that
emerged in Central
European culture right
at the moment when the
Euclidean understand-
ing of space as a contin-
uous, homogeneous, and
stable determinant of
the three-dimensional uni-
verse entered into crisis. *six* **Place: Permanence or Production**
Space could no longer be
conceived as an a priori category of perception, as Kant
was still able to affirm in his
Critique of Pure Reason, nor
could it be accepted as an
immutable datum, indissolubly
linked to the three perpendicular
coordinates of breadth, depth, and
height. As a consequence of this crisis, the concept of place, whose position in western culture had remained
essentially unaltered since Aristotelian
philosophy and Newtonian physics,
was also thrown into turmoil.

Einstein's theory of relativity substantially modified the modern notion of
space, associating it inseparably with that of
time and thereby determining a permanent
spatio-temporal mutability of the physical
world. Analogous phemomena soon followed in

the spheres of the arts and architecture: since cubism at least, the spatial and the temporal came to figure as two always interrelated variables. In the life sciences, too, Henri Poincaré established the deformability of perceived space so that, from the subject's point of view, it no longer made sense to continue to imagine a universe before which the observer could or even should attune his faculties of reception. Simultaneously, in the initial moments of the discipline of ecology, the theories of *Umwelt* propounded by Jakob von Uexküll undermined the stability of biological space by demonstrating that vegetable and animal life pursued their courses not in vast, limitless territories but between individuals and their environmentally determined spaces in such a way as to render the individual and his environment indistinguishable from one another.

For architecture, the notion of space is linked to the development of modernism. The idea that architecture is the production of post-Euclidean spaces, in accordance with the infinite repertoire of possibilities offered by modern physics, biology, and psychology, exactly parallels the developments to which we have just referred. It was Adolf von Hildebrand who confirmed the relativity of artistic space by demonstrating that our close and distance visions affect objectively different experiences of any work of art. It is the perception of space, therefore, that finally determines the nature of visual experience. Hildebrand's reasoning, subsequently developed by August Schmarsow and Aloïs Riegl, destroyed Gottfried Semper's explanation of the genesis of the arts on the basis of their material conditions. Schmarsow's notion of *Raumgefühl* established that the moment of perception could not be reduced to purely quantitative, material data. Movement, vision, and touch act together in the production of a global, sentimental experience, which means, for example, that the reality of a work of architecture is inseparable from human perception and its active mechanisms. Riegl subsequently developed the concept of *Kunstwollen*, or artistic will, determining that works of art were such not by virtue of their technical or geographical conditions or by the materials from which they were constructed, as Semper had thought, but as the products of a will—a subjective desire to manifest a vision of the world not through symbols or images but by means of new and changing spatial experiences.

This notion of architectonic space was adopted by avant-garde culture and criticism from Adolf Behne to Sigfried Giedion, from Frank Lloyd Wright to Mies van der Rohe, from Picasso to Duchamp. Their proposed spatial innovations were fundamental to the new art born out of the crisis of classicism. Space was no longer perceived as an initial datum, an a priori starting point upon which the architect's work intervened; instead, space itself resulted from an architectonic proposition. Space, and the infinite spatio-temporal experiences that the architect could create, became the final objects of architectural invention. They were not cause but consequence in a universe where relativity—not only physico-mathematical but biological, psychological, and philosophical as well—constituted an entirely new point of view.

This spatial creativity primarily manifested itself psychologically. Close and distant vision, touch, and bodily movement establish the conditions for the experience of space in such a way that the production of new spaces is indissolubly bound with the exploitation of the perceptual mechanisms of the human subject. In the same way that certain currents in the visual arts exploit extreme perceptual conditions in order to obtain new aesthetic effects—sleeplessness artificially stimulated by drugs in surrealism, or the mechanical optical experiences initiated by Duchamp—so too architecture was to find the road to spatial innovation expanded by the exploration of all possible psychological pathways.

But this seemingly expansive road took a momentous turn: the influences of *Neue Sachlichkeit* and functionalist techniques transformed it into a pathway of psychological empiricism. For these architects, human perception, experience, and needs could be codified purely mechanically. The cultural climate in the years following World War II confirmed this directional shift away from the notion of space as a production based on the psychological stimuli of the individual, setting into motion a lengthy process of revision only superficially legitimated by a return to empirical data. Psychological empiricism—most fundamentally, the development of Gestalt psychology—replaced Husserlian phenomenology. Consequently, the notion of *place* replaced that of *space*.

A new architectural sensibility manifested itself, critiquing the abstract character of the notion of space utilized up to then and, more generally, the mechanistic nature and purely invented origin of the spatial experiences that early modernism had put forth. In opposition to this abstraction, existentialism proposed putting into practice Edmund Husserl's maxim of a return to things in themselves. Architecture was expected to refer to the particular concrete conditions of each situation, obtained in precise space and time. The task of architecture was to build places in which to live. Just as there were no universal essences, only particular and concrete historical existences, neither were there any spaces created in vitro, any experiments of a general character. Instead, architecture was expected to interrupt the endless horizons of earth and sky, creating specifically determined, essentially defined qualities of place. These qualitative dimensions were essential. Architecture was to gather them together, making them visible, solid, and articulate. If man was the custodian of words, from which the meaning of things emerges, then architecture had a precise purpose: to transform the given conditions of place into *words* that would signify the qualities of existence, revealing the richness and content of each place's potential. This undertaking derived not from general principles nor from the vacuum of innovation. It emerged instead from earth and sky, light and shadow, and the site's ancestral images and histories. The work of architecture is no more than a patient recognition, a laborious cultivation of seeds that only await the hand of whomever is capable of making them grow and bear fruit.

The change that existentialism introduced into European and American architecture in the 1950s was far more radical than was then realized. Underlying an appearance of continuity were certain subtle generational shifts: first Aalto, followed by Nordic empiricism, Team X neoexistentialism, and Italian historicism. Each represented the triumph of history, structural complexity, environmentalism, and attention to particular qualities, over sweeping manifestoes and general assertions. In addition, each movement underscored the conviction that architecture was not so much a productive, industrial activity as a craft, necessarily bound up with the genius loci—the history, myths, symbolism, and signification of a place. Other lines of development sharing common roots with these existentially influenced architectural movements included Marcel and Mounier's personalism, Karl Jaspers's mental archaeologism, Maurice Merleau-Ponty's solipsism of language, and the study of the psychology of perception. All represent the disillusioned thought of a generation that, having lost all faith in grand visions, general principles, the future, or progress of any sort, advocated instead a philosophy of personal commitment.

Diffuse existentialism and the particularly determining influences of Martin Heidegger and Merleau-Ponty critically inflected the ideas of the modern movement by means of conceptual shifts that initially appeared to be innocuous but were actually imbued with the radical changes developed in the architectonic culture of the 1950s and 1960s. The historian and critic Christian Norberg-Schulz most clearly characterizes this position. From his now remote *Intentions* of 1963 to his significantly titled book *Genius Loci* of 1979, Norberg-Schulz's work extended Heidegger's inspiration. He analyzes architecture primarily as an activity that signals places. Place is recognition, delimitation, the establishment of confines. The genius loci is evidently a mythical divinity, a private demon that inhabits a particular site, which architecture makes manifest, celebrates, interrogates, and heeds. Geography and history join hands in the architectural place that precisely defines space and time. This notion of place corresponds to a continualist conception of the architectural process. Architecture's vocation lies in its service to the discovery of what already exists prior to it, as a permanent background against which it illuminates roots, outlines, and unvarying constants.

The most banal result of the postwar existentialist crisis has been a trivialization of historical styles. In Europe and America, however, there has also been a genuine, sincere return to languages determined by time and history that has produced a literally conservative culture of the city, imitative of the past and committed above all to recuperation, permanence, custody, and remembrance of the genius of the place. The notion of place as a central category has occupied a key position in the thinking of individuals as seemingly dissimilar as Aldo Rossi and Robert Venturi. Rossi has theorized architecture as a continual return to archetypes: permanent and immutable forms constituting the consistent identity underlying insignificant surface changes. The architecture of the city is, in structuralist terms, a clear demonstration of historical permanence. Before undertaking what should always be a hermeneutic task, the reading of a text already written, handed down by the past, the architect must recognize the morphological and typological analyses that form the substrata of place. For Venturi, contextualism similarly encourages no more than slight shifts of emphasis, and the survival of a species of diffuse classicism—popular, cultured, courtly, or domestic—is nothing other than the manifestation, in linguistic terms, of the central condition of architecture as a reflexive meditation on a world of already written words.

Today's context has changed substantially, however. Ours is a media culture where distances are reduced to the point of being virtually instantaneous, and where the reproduction of images by mechanisms of every kind has meant that an image is no longer linked to any one place but instead floats unattached across the length and breadth of the planet. While this ubiquitous society, this global village, generates experiences of simultaneity, multiple presence, and the constant generation of new stimuli, it has also produced feelings of profound estrangement. We are strangers in our own land, as Julia Kristeva has suggested, acknowledging the paradox that our modern universality simultaneously engenders expulsion and exile. Our art and literature return time and time again to the contemporary individual's experiences of loneliness and isolation. Nietzsche's resurgent influence over recent philosophy— a return initiated by Heidegger's later writings—provides yet one more indication that it is in the philosophy of negation and nihilism that contemporary culture recognizes itself.

The phenomenon of deconstructivism has proved highly illuminating. First emerging as a label dreamed up by American critics, it served for several years as the rallying point for certain common experiences in architecture that had nothing but the most metaphorical connection with the homonymous movement in literary criticism, centered around Jacques Derrida and the Yale school of literary criticism. Mark Wigley's introductory text to the 1988 "Deconstructivist Architecture" exhibition at MoMA acknowledged the distance between the two. He situated the architectural version close to the modern tradition, particularly as a reconsideration of the Russian constructivist legacy. In so-called deconstructive architecture, decomposition, distortion, and ambiguity are common values. These displacements mark a reaction against the structuralist order, the exhausting presence of archetypes, and continuity as a primary value in space and in historical consciousness. These deconstructivist architectures correspond both to the estranging context of our global village and to the destructive, negative energies that permeate a cultural situation in which the increasingly unsettling absence of principles becomes bearable only through private manifestations of resistance and individualism. The evident formalism that dominated this brief but significant architectonic phenomenon of the late 1980s reveals cultural emptiness and nihilism more than self-absorbed aestheticism. This somewhat hollow formalism signifies an experience of desolation, disorder, rupture, the unstoppable slipping away or dislocation of things. These are the metaphors for a void whose associations are with absences and disillusion in our contemporary political, religious, public, and personal spheres.

The writings of Blumberg, Cacciari, Trias, and the demythologizing theology of the disciples of Rudolf

Bultmann provide a second response to our contemporary context. Not only is God dead but the vacuum of his absence has created an inescapable whirlpool that has swallowed up collective commitment and moral reasoning, undermining architectural attempts to reestablish essential gestures, concern with human dwelling, and attention to the deeper meaning of the place. Recent architecture provides no places, no dwellings in which to halt and rest. The monuments for memory are archaeological ones, disconnected fragments only partially excavated, filled more with questionings and doubts than with comfortable presences.

The anthropologist Marcel Detienne has challenged the assumptions that underlie theories of place. In an extensive survey, ranging across a number of different present and historical cultures, he called into question the Heideggerian confidence in the existence of (and the necessity for) fixed points capable of organizing space and memory: "What is a place? Does it have a name? Is it something fixed? What does it mean to dwell? Do dwelling, ordering, constructing form a continuous chain? There are places that speak, others that act as signs, places that are like mouths to be fed, like bellies that have to be filled. There are free places, vacant, available. . . . First gestures, initial steps: to begin, to inaugurate, to establish." The notion of place appears to be indissolubly linked to the notion of time. Sites of historic cultures have frequently challenged time: monuments accumulate memory in defiance of oblivion, permanently evoking founding individuals, acts, or institutions. Place as foundation, as *fons*, as that which lies beneath, belongs to cultures that find their identity in the struggle against the passage of time, seeking to arrest time by means of ritual and myth. The architecture of these cultures becomes part of these rites of foundation, memory, and permanence.

But there is also a culture of the event: a culture that, in the moment of fluidity and decomposition leading toward chaos, is capable of generating instants of energy that from certain chaotic elements construct—out of the present and toward the future—a new fold in multiple reality. That which was many folds over on itself, manifesting an *any* that can arrive at a *one*. The event is a *vibration*, as Deleuze has written in an appraisal of Alfred North Whitehead's thinking. It is the undulation of an element that extends across those that follow it, establishing, like a light or sound wave, a system of harmonics in the air that subsist for a time before dissipating. But the event is also a point of encounter, a conjunction whereby the lines of a limitless itinerary cross with others to create nodal points of outstanding intensity. Finally, the event is a *grasping*, the action of a subject who, within the chaotic flux of events, arrests those moments that most attract or impel, in order to hold on to them. It is a subjective action, producing a moment of pleasure and fragile plenitude. Although the event is always something that takes place in a global disorder devoid of meaning, this happy moment—at times accidental, at times the result of a willing intellect—constitutes an outstanding instant in a constant flux, a harmonious, polyphonic chord in a situation of permanent transition.

The forceful images of Deleuze's thinking—the nomadic, the war machine, the rhizome—point toward the tantalizingly provocative idea of an architecture of the event. In a world that incessantly consumes images, in a constantly expanding metropolitan culture, in a universe whose buildings are no more than a few of the infinite number of figurative and informative dwellings that surround us, there nonetheless exists the architectonic event. This event is like an extended chord, like an intensity at an energetic crux of streams of communication, a subjective apprehension offered by the architect in the joy of producing a polyphonic instant in the heart of the chaotic metropolis.

Jean-François Lyotard has provided an acute explanation of the opposition between the notion of the sublime, belonging to modern aesthetics, and the notion of beauty, belonging to classical culture. This opposition, investigated by Kant in his *Critique of Judgment*, signifies for Lyotard the contrast between an Aristotelian aesthetics whose ultimate goal was moral elevation and another aesthetic experience whose sole objective is to capture intensity. In classical culture, beauty was linked to the splendor of the world order, as well as to the essential apprehension of the truth of things. For western metaphysics since Aristotle, the true, the good, and the beautiful have been interwoven and are therefore inseparable. In modern times, however, since Edmund Burke and Immanuel Kant, the sublime constitutes another form of aesthetic experience that is, once more, pure event: something new that, even if only for an instant, fictively produces a parallel world, a *Zwischenwelt*, as Paul Klee called it. Out of the essential indeterminacy of the conflictive and changing modern world, art opens up spaces of visual, auditory, or emotional intensity, hoping to bring about a shock, an experience stripped of references, disarmed in relation to the imitation of nature. Only the intensity of this shock guarantees the potency of the avant-garde work of art. Pure event as the result of a deliberate action.

The places of present-day architecture cannot repeat the permanences produced by the force of the Vitruvian *firmitas*. The effects of duration, stability, and defiance of time's passing are now irrelevant. The idea of place as the cultivation and maintenance of the essential and the profound, of a genius loci, is no longer credible in an age of agnosticism; it becomes reactionary. Yet the loss of these illusions need not necessarily result in a nihilistic architecture of negation. From a thousand different sites the production of place continues to be possible. Not as the revelation of something existing in permanence, but as the production of an event. It is not a question of producing an ephemeral, instantaneous, fragile, fleeting architecture. What these lines seek to defend is the value of places produced out of the meeting of present energies, resulting from the force of projective mechanisms capable of promoting intense, productive shock.

The contemporary place must form a crossroads, and the contemporary architect must have the talent to apprehend it as such. Place is not a ground, keeping faith with certain images; nor is it the strength of the topography or of archaeological memory. Place is, rather, a conjectural foundation, a ritual of and in time, capable of fixing a point of particular intensity in the universal chaos of our metropolitan civilization.

HERZOG & de MEURON.

Values such as reason, logic, economy, democracy, and progress have been so widely disseminated that they have become mere phonemes whose significance is at best doubtful and whose foundations are unstable. Paradoxically, the modern processes of diffusion and consumption have voided of content precisely those values that, in a form of cultural leveling, they have made ubiquitous. Now is not the moment to engage in philosophical reflection as a means of diagnosing our present situation. The malady is evident enough: our age lacks any clear system of values whose validity is sufficiently and widely acknowledged as to serve as the basis for those practical activities—such as the production of art and architecture—that provide tangible manifestation of the dominant ideas within a given civilization.

Yet art and architecture continue to be produced. Although radical critics claim that contemporary attempts at articulating social values through art or architecture inevitably fail for want of such values, I would claim otherwise. My aim is to investigate how works of art *loaded* with signification can indeed be created during this period of crisis. In other words, my intention is to analyze certain recent architectures precisely as endeavors to construct not a building but a *meaning* that reflects the precariousness of the present situation: the dispersion of values and the absence of unshakable, foundational referents.

With Friedrich Nietzsche the secure certainty of the Enlightenment project was destroyed, and with it the confidence that the subject's relationship to the world was fluid, stable, and ultimately constructive. Neither the positivist objectivist scientists, who upheld the nineteenth century's scientific and technological revolutions, nor Hegel's positing of a subject whose dialectical growth absorbed the objective world into the unstoppable onward march of Absolute Spirit, were convincing when they proclaimed the decline of Greco-Christian culture. The world is will and representation—to borrow Arthur Schopenhauer's expression—and the subject is no longer transcendental. Rather, it has become an empirical being thrown into the world of existentialist thought.

At the end of the twentieth century, with both the confidence in scientific and technological progress and the values of the subject shattered, art and architecture are resting on the precarious foundations of their desolation. Their displacement corresponds to the terms of experience and the propositions of the empirical subject, that sensitive witness to the loss of totality, capable only of transmitting relative, partial, individual contents from the fragile limitations of their conditions. The most sensitive architecture of the present moment is thus no longer the expression of a communal project that transmits the values of rationality, progress, and collective emancipation to the urban landscape, but is instead merely the modest presence of particular discourses that publicly expose what should only be regarded as private experience. With the decline of *grands projets* and civic patronage systems, private experience provides the last resort for establishing a weak but respectable veracity.

These premises provide the basis from which I would like to analyze two well-known types of recent architectonic experience. Although widely diverse, both approaches engage the crisis of values referred to above, and can only be understood as individual responses to the contemporary situation. But while the two approaches are similar in the individualism of their respective responses, their ways of manifesting this individualism differ greatly.

The undermining of the theoretical foundations of the modern movement led to an anxious search for things past, a Proustian *recherche du temps perdu*. Over a number of years, practicing architects have promoted the proliferation of historiographical exercises of every description in an effort to reestablish some kind of repertoire of objective, transhistorical codes. The hope is that these types and models could act as foundations for an understanding both of the places on which to build and of the references in terms of which this new construction is to be configured. Morphology and typology seemed to have installed themselves at the center of a refounded theory, with the expectation that they might enable practice to escape the arbitrary and the idiotic. Our experience of that constructed foundation, however, has revealed that it is perhaps less innocent than its formulation might have suggested. Understanding it as what the philosopher Miguel Morey has called a form of higher psychopathology, we can apprehend quite other significations, leading us from a consideration of the objective to the subjective.

In the first place, as poststructuralism has demonstrated in other cultural fields, the recomposition of the entire history of architecture on the basis of these phantasmagorias implies positioning the subject before the overwhelming weight of a past time. Conventional historiography is capable of understanding this temporal tonnage only in terms of organic evolutionism, in the sense of a limitless process of ever more valuable transformations. I use the term *phantasmagoria* here according to its precise definition in the psychology of classical thought: *phantasmata* are the figurative projections by means of which undefined states of anxiety or desire are synthesized. Similarly, these architectonic types and models are used to synthesize divergent references to past time. This truly Proustian architectural *recherche* of past time results in a cultural situation that has lost once and for all the experience of historicity as an enveloping reality within which the subject, incorporated into a wider and more objective reality, can feel comforted.

In its clumsiest and most banal forms, this research into the past rapidly descends to the reactionary historicist level of that architecture commonly known as postmodern. In its more intelligent versions, however, when it clearly and actively opposes postmodern sentimentality and commercialism, it becomes what I propose to call the architecture of repetition and difference.

It should not come as a surprise that in the field of philosophy, the problems of repetition and difference have commanded the attention of a wide range of contemporary thinkers. From Martin Heidegger to Jacques Derrida, Hans-Georg Gadamer to Jürgen Habermas, Emmanuel Levinas, Gianni Vattimo, or Gilles Deleuze, repetition and difference suggest questions that are directly linked to the problem of the subject and the possibility of an ontological foundation for modern thought.

What has this question of repetition and difference meant in recent architecture, if not the constant problematizing with which the new work of architecture can establish itself precisely at the crossroads of these two opposed terms?

In an act of constructing that presents itself as contingent, as something unnecessary yet at the same time desired, the contemporary architect, in her or his solitude, individually confronts history. Their encounter will not be ingenuously contextual or facilely imitative, but a solitary rendezvous made before the specters, the phantasmata, of Architecture. When analyzing a particular place, the architect will encounter a simulacrum in personal memory—through strictly autobiographical episodic suggestions—of a trace on the basis of which he or she can establish the *difference* that avoids *repetition*. Or, as Deleuze would have it, the architect will invert Platonism, that is to say, will deny the primacy of the original over the remembrance of its image.

The highly intelligent works of Aldo Rossi, Michael Graves, Rafael Moneo, Mario Botta, and so many others are valuable contemporary architectures that should no longer be understood as applications of an understanding of history and its deep structures—as repetition—but rather as propositions framed from the unbridgeable distance between the contemporary condition of architectural culture and the historical and modern tradition of architecture from the past—as difference. It is necessary to establish that the mechanism of repetition and difference that underlies works of this type is exclusively the result of an operation that begins and ends in the subject. This result reproduces for us a metaphorical image of the subject's own recollection, bathed in the solitude of the anguished situation where all lessons of history have apparently been discarded, and nothing other than individual talent has replaced history to provide guidance for the architect.

In recent years European *arte povera* has been the vehicle by means of which the visual arts have sent out a message of a poetic indigence valuing at every turn the evocative residues of objects that serve as archetypes of art and daily life. So too this architecture of repetition and difference has aligned itself with the reworked, stylized imaginary of some moment in the history of architecture. This is not historicism. Nor is it the facile marketing of signifying elements. It is an elborate operation in and from which the subject establishes the radical sense of difference, the modern distance between the present and any past, and the elaborate figuration of a repetition that seeks to evoke an impossible permanent world of the architectonic essential.

Alongside this attitude, forged in the tension generated from the subject between the impossible and the necessary, another and different poetics develops itself: that which the philosopher Eugenio Trias has described as the logic of the limit.

Characteristics that define the modern artwork provide that a process of mediation is set into motion once the synthetic condition has been attained in the work itself: form and idea become mutually dependent as the artwork seeks to be at once concrete object and sensible manifestation of an idea. This is the Hegelian logic that leads art to its own eclipse, to its death in design, advertising, fashion, or building. Architecture, the original symbolic art, would thus have died in modernity at the hands of its need to estrange itself, in a collective rationality that subsumes it in something that at once annihilates and transcends it. The objective experience of the death of art, of the end of architecture, is as certain as the necessity of Hegelian dialectics. It occurs in objective fashion in late capitalism, where architecture is diluted into speculative development, or the techniques of advertising, or arguments of state. But it is no less certain that this situation leads into a new process of refounding architecture as the renewed experience of certain basic data of conduct and perception.

Just as there has been a subjective refounding of architecture on its historic structures, there has also been a movement of new foundation based on the elementary data of experience.

What separates minimalist art from *arte povera* is the fact that the former sets out from elementary synesthetic experiences (geometry, color, space), while the latter reelaborates, in the way we noted above, existing iconography, especially that which proceeds from an understanding of history and of the experience accumulated by memory. Artistic minimalism constitutes an ambitious refounding of the visual arts. Its intent is clear: to draw back to the limits. Its method is to carry aesthetic and thus significative experience to the frontiers of the insignificant and the obvious. This degree zero of aesthetic signification is generally resolved in a reductive manner, based primarily on abstraction and on opening up the fissure of signification by those slight gestures, movements, or events that the subject is incapable of eliminating, that is, incapable of removing from the *limes*, the limit.

The limit is a place defined only by the opposition between an institutionalized center, powerful and technologized, and a periphery that dissolves away into virgin territory, uncontrolled and empty. The limit exists by virtue of the tension between those who wish to instrumentalize it and the indefinite into which it disappears. Minimalism is the experience of the limit in a reflected dimension. It is to be consciously in the limit, through the will to distance oneself from the center and through the effort to disappear into territories that have never been cultivated. The limit is a subjective experience. There are no limits that are fixed once and for all. The limit emerges at the very moment when the individual experience is made, approaching it at the risk of one's own identity. The limit does not constitute a program susceptible to generalization. It is not a response to the technical needs of society or the city. It offers no prospects, no perspectives of the future.

Just as there is a minimalist art that defines itself precisely by its proximity to the limit, there is also an architecture capable of risking itself in a venturing toward the degree zero of geometrical and spatial conformation. In the laconic architectures of Herzog and de Meuron, in the reductionism of Souto de Moura or Juan Navarro Baldeweg, in the controlled gesturality of Garcés and Sòria, in the strict monumentality of Francesco Venezia or Roberto Collovà, we discover a refounding of architecture as far removed from modern efficacy as from postmodern historical memory.

In many of these architects' buildings, what establishes signification is neither the context nor the tectonicity, neither the sense of place nor the typological or figurative references to other architectures of the past. They do not set out to affirm themselves through this remembering. Their architecture is, in a sense, much more immediate, direct, perceptible by means of the synesthetic experimentation of those who contemplate it.

In the same way that a piece by Dan Flavin or Donald Judd is lacking in references (at least in the sense of a process through which to produce the signification), these architectures also make themselves present, in the first instance, through the strict materiality of their volumes and materials. Further signification derives from the tension present in these material structures, in which some vibration is always inscribed, some slight gesture, an almost casual distortion, the fracturing of some geometry. In short, by the experience that the form cannot be reduced to a zero point and that the signification, not existing in the void, instead becomes intense at the moment when it is granted only a liminal space, a minimal appearance.

That this descent to the foundations (or vertiginous approximation to the limits) is an individual experience, embraced at the subject's own risk and disappearing the instant that one seeks to make it extensive, massive, or commercial, is an essential datum. In the contemporary crisis, the architecture of the limit is the most fragile and the surest path leading back to the encounter with the profound aesthetic experience, that is to say the technics and poetics, *technē* and *poiēsis*, of architecture.

A mere glance at re-
cent architectural pro-
duction and reception
confirms that the
architecture known as
high tech has developed
into the "serious" alter-
native to both the now
exhausted banality of
postmodernist classicism
and the laboratory experi-
mentalism of the so-called
deconstructivists. Of course   *eight*
all of these terms are impre-
cise, products of the conventions fostered by fashionable
critical tendencies. But if we
examine the facts in greater
depth, we can see that amid the
present situation's confusion and
turbulence, those architectures
that have chosen to adopt visible
high technology as their characteristic feature are gaining daily in
acceptance and prestige, not only
among practitioners but in the opinion of the wider public as well.

There is nothing new about
emphasizing the relationship between
technology and architecture; nor is there
anything new in the suggestion that contemporary architecture can be characterized
as the product of new technologies. On the
contrary, there is a genuine tradition of the new,

as Harold Rosenberg would put it, according to which innovation in architecture reflects the technical innovation that inspired it. From Gottfried Semper's progressive thinking to Eugène Viollet-le-Duc onward, the relationship between technology and architecture has assumed an increasingly primary role. Having abandoned the discourse of style, the architecture of modern times is characterized by its capacity to take advantage of the specific achievements of that same modernity: the innovations offered it by present-day science and technology. The relationship between new technology and new architecture even comprises a fundamental datum of what are referred to as avant-garde architectures, so fundamental as to constitute a dominant albeit diffuse motif in the figuration of new architectures.

This tradition of the modern movement seems to have been based on the following conceptual model: New technologies form the starting point for new architectures. Successive technical innovations spur successive innovations in architecture. So-called high technology developments thereby constitute the origin of the architecture of the same name. But in the general context of the crisis of the modern project—the loss of faith in innovation and progress—it is quite exceptional to find an architectural tendency whose basis lies in an affirmation of the modern project.

If, on the one hand, modernism's Enlightenment origins, now being called into question by thinkers such as Gianni Vattimo, Gilles Deleuze, and Jean Baudrillard, suggest that it is science—that is to say, the rational progress of man and society—that brings about technological innovation; and if, at the same time, it is technological innovation that sustains the progress of architecture, then we must conclude that the aim of high tech architecture is a modernization of the modern project—optimistic, scientific, and supposedly rational—that has developed over two centuries within the context of western culture. But the relations between technology, progress, and architecture are not, nor have they ever been, as simple as they first might seem.

In 1923, Le Corbusier published *Vers une architecture*, described in 1965 by Peter Collins as "the most influential book in 20th century architecture." As we know, this book-cum-manifesto of the ideals of modern architecture is, in reality, a montage, compiled from a series of articles published by Le Corbusier during 1920 and 1921 in the journal *L'Esprit Nouveau*. Throughout the book's seven chapters, Le Corbusier structures a complex meditation in which the issue of new technology occupies a central position. He poses the structure of the new architecture's global, technological discourse in the book's three primary sections: "Three Reminders to Architects," "Eyes Which Do Not See," and "Architecture."

The three chapters of "Three Reminders to Architects" concern the confrontation between engineering and architecture. Rather than apologize for modern engineering's radical submission to economy and calculation, architecture is presented as pure spiritual production. The forms and relationships established by architecture are distinguished from the strict forms of engineering with the assertion that in the latter, innovation is forever dictated by science and technology. Architecture, in contrast, for all that it learns from the engineers' way of working, should seek a different role for itself: expression of the absolute. Analyzing Le Corbusier's position, it is possible to discern a cautious reaction to the radical technologism sustained by the materialism of the avant-garde, specifically by the Russian constructivists-productivists and the German *Neue*

Sachlichkeit. What initially appears to be a pamphlet argu-
ing that modern engineering should serve as a guiding
principle for the new architecture emerges as an expression
of a dialectic between identity and difference, between
engineering and architecture.

The chapters of "Eyes Which Do Not See" clearly
argue that the new architecture should follow engineering's
lead in the design and processes of great machines, structures, and the production line. Ships, planes, automobiles,
turbines, silos, and mechanized furniture are all presented
in the pages of *Vers une architecture* as the icons of modern
civilization. But then the sections "The Lesson of Rome,"
"The Dynamic of the Plan," and "Architecture" define
architecture as pure creation of the spirit. How are we to
understand this constant dialectic within Le Corbusier's
text?

We might say that for the architect of the Villa Savoye,
architecture constitutes a mediation: that is, an operation
of signification through which the new technological universe is incorporated into (without constituting the ultimate objective of) architectonic manifestation. We have to
bear in mind that in the text we are examining, architecture is not technology, nor engineering, yet neither is it historical form. Both then and now, architecture is the
mediation between the techniques, the images, and the
panorama that culture presents at every instant, which Le
Corbusier calls the order of the universe. The ultimate
architectural objective is a mediation between the technical and the aesthetic. Although manifested on the practical, productive, particular plane of objects, architectural
mediation is exercised on the plane of discourse, expression, and message.

The objective of architecture is not the literal illustra-
tion of functions or techniques, but the eloquent exposition,

the convincing presentation, the credible manifestation of the message of universality that can be found in those techniques. Eloquence, conviction, and credibility are the objectives of the art of rhetoric, the creative act of effectively communicating a message. Architecture as mediation is rhetoric, the art of communication and eloquence.

This understanding of the mediating effect of architecture suggests a fundamental objective for architecture. The book we are analyzing closes with a chapter whose title initially appears to be out of place: "Architecture or Revolution." We might regard the question as extemporaneous if we failed to appreciate the dichotomy that Le Corbusier here advances. For the revolution is not so much the social unrest or the violent change that can be produced by the masses as it is, above all, the insecurity and fear, the disorder and the threat represented by the forces of the technico-scientific revolution if they are not brought into line, if their blind energy is not mediated.

This dilemma between architecture and revolution is the translation of that dialogic optimism in which Le Corbusier glories throughout his entire production—an optimism in which scientific and technical changes need not be regarded as threateningly inhuman, dangerously destructive of the individual and the life of society, but rather as beneficent products capable of reconciling subject and environment through the introduction of architecture as mediator.

Art, theory, and criticism in the years between the wars were, to a great degree, suspicious and fearful of the new technologies, mass production, and the increasing automation of vital processes. If we consider the literature, cinema, or philosophy of those years, we find a reiterated and obsessive preoccupation with the new, unfolding mechanical and technical world. In H. G. Wells, George

Orwell, and Aldous Huxley, the apocalyptic vision of the future is taken to be the only conceivable respite in light of the unstoppable process of the technical sophistication of the social and private life of modern metropolitan man. Even those apparently convinced eulogists of the new man of technical civilization, such as Ernst Jünger, found it impossible to overlook the profound emotional instability provoked by these new situations in work and in war.

What was needed was to find something that did not yet exist in order for the new power to be not a threat but an instrument of individual and collective growth. This is precisely the attitude expressed by Heidegger in confronting the problem of *Technik*, which occupies a central position in his reflections in the years before and after the Second World War. The historic rupture between doing and being, between *technē* and *poiēsis* is, in Heidegger, the expression of an essential malaise in modern man and society. The cure for this malaise lies in art: in building, dwelling, and thinking.

While Georg Simmel, Walther Rathenau, Martin Wagner, Peter Behrens, Sigfried Giedion, and Ernst May were proclaiming an inevitable adherence to the technified world of the twentieth century, fear and dread were no less surely taking hold of artists and intellectuals, overshadowing the optimism of the intellectual and artistic avant-garde. Celibate surrealist machines, absurd Chaplinesque parodies of Taylorism, architectonic expressionism set up against the horror of industrial society, provide some of the evidence that the relationship between the new technology and progress was not everywhere experienced as something evident and almost natural.

Even Le Corbusier could not regard this relationship as an unmediated, unequivocal sign of progress. On the contrary, for him there was a need for mediation: that is, a need to eradicate errors of every kind between the new technology and the social order, which for him was to be found in architecture; a need to subsume the new technical and social situation by means of specifically artistic operations. In a word, what was needed was *rhetoric*, according to the definition that I propose here: a positive, apposite contribution to the creation of a language, as well as the explication of a reality that refuses to be appropriated without its mediation.

In 1962, Alan Colquhoun published an article in *Architectural Design* that distinguished between the literal and the symbolic in the technical aspects of modern architecture. This distinction was in a sense parallel to the one drawn by Colin Rowe and Robert Slutzky in their memorable text "Transparency: Literal and Phenomenal" of 1956, where they established an absolute difference between literal transparency and phenomenal transparency. In these two texts, each concerned with different problems—technology or transparency—that were issues in modern architecture, the authors established the difference between immediate, obvious, evident signification and a signification that is only intelligible in terms of a *mechanism* of signification. To the immediacy of the literal signification they opposed the mediation of an entire linguistic system, by virtue of which such typically rhetorical devices as metaphor, redundancy, and eurythmics entered into architectural play.

An example of the literal presentation of the relationship between technology and architecture in the period of transition between the first and second machine ages (in Reyner Banham's phrase) can be found in the celebrated proposals of the inventor Buckminster Fuller. The work of this autodidact, in the tradition of Giedion's *Mechanization Takes Command*, provides the best example of an immediate relationship between technology and architecture, if the term architecture can indeed be applied to the artifacts he produced. By means of simplified exegeses of certain problems—urban movement, transport, flexibility, unitary control of climate, etc.—Fuller created a whole repertoire of artifacts that both depicted and demonstrated recent technology. Each of his inventions was a unidirectional response to a well-defined problem; each effectively simplified the multiple facets of the problem itself. The outcome was his houses, automobiles, compact bath systems, mobile housing units, all covered by the trade name Dymaxion. None of these objects relied upon qualities of complexity, permanence, and the relationship with place. These were artifacts in which, as in war machines, the objective to be achieved had been deliberately simplified with the aim of presenting in the most obvious manner the immediate relationship between necessity and technological response. What might have been seen as an extension of that technico-scientific pioneering spirit exemplified by the inventions of Jules Verne became instead the paradigm of a relationship considered to be the ultimate expression of the modern ideal: the felicitous meeting of technology and architecture.

When, in the sixties, the Archigram group developed an architecture free of inhibitions from the point of view of the incorporation of new technologies, Bucky Fuller was hailed as the guru of all the neo-avant-garde radicalisms that heralded the crisis of the modern movement. Archigram enriched Fuller's precedent with the introduction of many other parameters into the process. Probably the most important of these was that all of their formal repertoires subscribed to a mediate conception of architectural production. These repertoires were drawn from the imagery of such state-of-the-art technologies as space rockets, deep-sea oil platforms, motor homes, domestic appliances, and the accelerated consumption of images produced by television. All of these ingredients were brought together in architectural proposals that, consciously "alternative" as they aimed to be, exalted mobility in counterpoint to the traditional stability of historic buildings; exhalted the colors and forms of pop culture in opposition to the repertoires and canons of conventional architecture; exhalted the mass media message in place of the institutionalized communication inherent in the architecture of the past.

Accumulation, montage, containment, change, multiplicity of impulses, tension, and immediacy were some of the values put forward in the ironic and at times utopian drawings and projects of a series of architects for whom offering an alternative to the established architecture—not only the classical but also, by this time, the modern establishment—was as important as was the need to respond to the new technical, mechanical, and electronic age. Architecture, once again, was seeking to express the spirit of its time—a truly modern condition that was not to be achieved through any adherence to formal repertoires, but through the perpetually renewed encounter between new technologies and architectural artifacts.

The theorists of this renewed optimism between technology and architecture were to be found first in Britain in the circle that formed around the Independent Group, which included the Smithsons, Richard Hamilton, Eduardo Paolozzi, and the young James Stirling and Colin St. John Wilson. From the theoretical point of view, the most outstanding member of this group was undoubtedly Reyner Banham, for his influence extended from the mid-fifties throughout the sixties. With a solid academic background in the Courtauld Institute, Banham's doctoral thesis on the architecture of the first machine age specifically offered an overview of the fiasco of the programmatic intentions of the greats of the modern movement in their failed attempt to establish an architecture that would respond directly to the conditions of the mechanized contemporary world.

In criticizing the lack of substance in that relationship during the first machine age, Banham implicitly proposed that it should be the second machine age, in other words the period about which he was writing, that would finally establish an intimate relationship between machine and architecture. The position Banham occupied was that of a call for orthodoxy, if by orthodoxy we are to understand the need to invent the architecture of the present age as the outcome of a mechanistic civilization. Marshall McLuhan completed this theoretical picture with an affirmation of communication by means of images as the new core of reality in a culture that had moved from the production of objects to the production of messages. The call to pansemiotic conversion provided, in McLuhan, the theoretical support for the production of ephemeral, instant, changing, purely communicational architectures.

In contrast to this perspective that envisioned a newborn architecture springing directly from equally new technological conditions, we find the more somber analyses of that same technological situation in the investigations of, among others, the Situationists and related groups, such as Cobra and the International Lettriste. The only point of contact between these movements and the apologists of the new technical context was their common use of mass culture as the material for their reflections. But while in the pop climate of Archigram, or later in Venturi's McLuhanism, the new situation was assessed in a fundamentally positive manner, Situationism concentrated on exposing the poverty and banality of what Guy Debord called the "society of the spectacle." In the same way that, in the years between the wars, philosophers and historians of art and architecture had sought to rationalize the uncontrolled, frightening impact of mechanization by focusing on its positive aspects, so too in the boom years of the fifties and sixties there was forceful criticism of the mass urbanism of the new suburbs, of the indiscriminate consumption of objects and images, and of the alienation of collective life. This criticism took the form of calls for individual liberation, for the reconstruction of private living space, and for the privileged experience of situations, instant events in which, within a limited time span, it was possible for individuals to rediscover themselves. In Situationism, the theory of the *dérive* represented not the positive valorization of some organized, clear, and simple spatial experience, but the richness of an erratic drifting, of mobility with no predefined goal, of possibilities for personal enrichment in the context of modern urban living.

Another type of critique to emerge from this same situation, from what Alain Touraine has called the postindustrial society, was constituted by the growing ecology movement. In origin antiurban and antitechnological, the ecologists directed their critical gaze at the *parte maudite* of the affluent society: the misery of its detritus, the uncontrolled chaos of its waste products, and the limitless consumption of resources and energy as harbingers of a new holocaust. Perhaps the most immediate consequence of the ecology movement was the exploration of alternative energy sources, materials, and also architectures. It is beyond the scope of the present text, however, to analyze all the consequences of the direct application of the theoretical propositions of ecologism in the architecture of the last twenty years. What this essay does seek to do is to indicate the theoretical context that the new technological situation in the western world has provoked in certain recent architectures.

The mission that so-called high tech architecture seems to have chosen for itself is precisely that of responding positively, with prophetic optimism, to the need for a reconstructed relationship between new technology and new architecture, as well as to the possibility, in certain cases, of taking up the critiques framed by the Situationists or ecologists by putting forth clean, energy-controlled architectures that would, in short, offer comfort and happiness to the user. It is surprising to note, time and again, that the observations made by Richard Rogers, Norman Foster, or Jean Nouvel, to mention only the better-known names, express a far greater concern with demonstrating the ecological and communicative values in their work than in defending technology as an adaptation to the spirit of the modern age. In the first place, these architects present their work as lying on the margins of that crisis which, from Jürgen Habermas to Jean Baudrillard, has been called postmodern. Theirs is an architecture in continuity with Gaudí, Mies, Le Corbusier, and Aalto, but also, and equally easily, with Buckminster Fuller and Archigram.

The innovation these architectures seek to offer lies not merely in construction, that is, in the application of new mechanical possibilities, but above all in communication and management. For all the architects of this tendency, the most marked emphasis is placed, on the one hand, on the effectiveness with which the new artifact explains its function, exhibits its objectives, and reveals the logic of its technique. This is the triumph of communication by way of an architecture of transparency and of increasing immateriality. On the other hand, much is made of the approach to the running of the project that results in such sophisticated, such perfect artifacts. Business techniques, management techniques, interdisciplinary collaboration, and the new approach to the division of labor would appear to be the keys to explaining this architecture's novelty and modernity.

Ideologically, this whole conceptual apparatus results in a clearly defined rhetorical message. In a world full of conflict such as ours in these final years of the twentieth century, such architectures present themselves, in the first place, as something obvious, evident, logical, rational, and economical. What greater poignancy than that of the victory of wisely administered technique? A victory is arrived at by way of paths signposted as traditionally conservative: social integration, professionalism, a white-coated architecture. Here, complete felicity is consummated. All ecological imbalance seems to have disappeared, and high production and maintenance costs are forgotten in favor of images of adaptation to the landscape, to people's work, and to urban integration. High tech architecture is not, according to this reading, something closed in on itself, but rather the route by which the social goals of a highly developed culture are sought through the rationality of wisely utilized technologies.

The result is a rhetorical exaltation of the institutions or, more specifically, of the big corporations in whom the tremendously costly production of these great artifacts finds its staunchest allies. Much more than the public sector or the private universe of house and home, the privileged space for high tech architecture is that of the great monopoly enterprises, the multinational companies that represent the de facto powers of the most highly developed capitalist societies. Paradoxically, what was in its origins a pioneering, avant-garde attitude has now come to constitute, in accordance with the discourse of the modern tradition, a rhetorical exaltation of technology precisely as the road leading to personal and social pacification. In this we see the fulfillment of the permanent vocation of technological rhetoric, in the positive meaning of the word: the art of eloquence with which a message—here an integrating message—is framed by the creator of architectural form. We are concerned here with a rhetoric that, once again, demonstrates the quality we have observed right from the origins of this aporia of the modern. It is a rhetoric that can be literal or mediated, an immediate translation of technological icons accumulated as a redundant call to their legitimization, or an elaborated architecture in which the repertoires offered by technology serve to mediate in terms of rules, protocols, and codifications that culminate in the construction of an elaborate system of communication through architecture.

It would not be difficult to uncover, in the work of Norman Foster, the most thoroughly elaborated high tech architecture: a whole painstaking procedure by means of which his buildings are increasingly produced as genuinely "mediatic" architectures. They are mediatic in part because of their use of the mass media, and in part by virtue of their mediated process. Between the gross datum of the state-of-the-art technology adopted and the final architectonic result, there lies an entire procedure—knowledgeable and elaborate—of typological definition that is as valid for the large-scale decisions as for those concerned with details, furnishings, or complementary elements.

Union, tension, lightness, provisionality, flexibility, juxtaposition of scales of intervention, continuity, transparency: these are the predominant criteria that seem to offer themselves as a metamorphosis of the Vitruvian principles of *utilitas, firmitas, venustas.*

For many architects, the addiction to the continuity of the modern project never comes to more than an inarticulate stammering of mechanistic clichés. In Foster's work, however, we can see over the years the extent to which the technological approach has grown steadily more articulate and more syntactically rich. There is nothing else in the present panorama so elaborate or so coherent with the principle of adaptation between new technologies and new architectures. What would be paradoxical, if it were not so evidently effective, is the fact that his architecture is ultimately the most refined manifestation of conservative ideology and the most stable support of established society.

In contrast to the critical pathos, the nonconformity that runs through other currents in modernism, Foster's architecture suggests that the most refined rhetoric the world of technology presently offers us through the mediation of architecture should be precisely the most effective antidote to the fear and insecurity that unlimited technical development continues to incite in the majority of individuals.

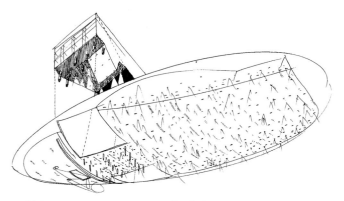

CIELING VIEW FOR THE PRESENCE OF ROOF

FRESH AIR   HOLE   } WILL ARRANGED WITH ITS OWN LOGIC.
EXOST AIR   HOLE   EACH HOLE HAS ITS OWN ENTITY OF THE LAY-OUT ON CIELING.
LIGHT   HOLE   MEANS   "
FIRE PERFORATION HOLE   } ROOF IS **ONE** ENTITY.
COLUMNS

According to Walter Benjamin, his "The Work of Art in the Age of Mechanical Reproduction," published in Pierre Klossowski's French translation in 1936, set out to "understand the impact of the changes of functions to which art in general is subject in the spasms of social evolution." In one *nine* sense, the essay is Benjamin's most expansive reflection on the reaction of the avant-garde—Dadaist, constructivist, surrealist—to the widespread conviction of the death of art and its substitution by another type of operation whose new conditions of production and reception directly resulted from the social, perceptual, and communicative conditions of modern capitalism. While Benjamin's unfinished *Passagenwerk* is devoted to the archaeology of that same modernity, chronicling the eclipse of dioramas, feuilletons, interiors, and world exhibitions in anticipation of what developed capitalism would bring about, "The Work of Art in the Age of Mechanical Reproduction" explicitly formulates the anticipated conditions and characteristics of the new

The Work of Architecture in the Age of Mechanical Reproduction

technical arts. Although Benjamin's analysis of art is concerned above all with its reception—distracted versus attentive; tactile versus optical—many of his observations regarding cinematography also serve to illuminate the conditions of production of modern art, and thus the new significations produced by these conditions.

The shooting of a film, especially a sound film, offers previously utterly inconceivable possibilities. The specific feature of this innovation lies in the technical process, and in the mediation between the filmed reality and the cinematographic projection. Benjamin explains the difference between the two with the resonantly suggestive analogy of the magician and the surgeon. The magician attempts to cure by means of the authority of his own individual personality, and by virtue of the special power that he represents; the surgeon, on the other hand, operates upon the patient, that is to say, he employs a technical procedure that is both objective and impersonal: decisive in each one of the contacts the surgeon establishes with the body he seeks to cure, but far removed from any idea of positioning himself as a whole subject before another whole subject. The new technical condition, product of the new social division of work, defines the manner by which action is produced. Only the coordination of these direct actions on the patient will lead to a successful surgical result.

Today's work of architecture is no longer the result of a magical action, but is produced in the first place by the social division of work, and secondly by the precise determination of technical characteristics: dimensions and materials. The building results from a manipulation that is controlled in each and every one of the phases of the process that leads to its production.

The contemporary architect is responsible not only for certain formal and technical decisions but also for putting a process in motion: one that is complex, articulated, and involves numerous operators who act directly on specific parts of the architectonic object. Historically, architecture's technical and material stability allowed the architect to operate as a medium, as a magician capable of formulating general hypotheses and essential formal decisions with the confidence that their materialization could be undertaken without the least difficulty. The degree of integration of the various technical procedures of building made these mere steps in an immediate relationship between the person who formulated the original idea and the final result.

If the social division of architectural work tends to take many of the tasks to be performed out of the hands of the architect, it simultaneously makes her or him responsible for the mediation, that is to say, the multiple, uncoordinated, technical maneuvers, each with its discontinuous logic and each carried out by specialists who have no grasp of their overall integration. The work of the architect, in some new sense, is that of producing the coordinated action of these disparate technical mechanisms. The idea, or the diagnosis, is worth nothing if the architectural project does not engage in its every detail these multiple fragments. The social division of work has broken the one-time practical unity of architecture from project through to completed object.

Montage—the cutting or the assembly—has become the central operation for both filmic and architectural production. The architect is no longer, as the painter still is, someone who produces in person, directly. The project is a complex document that describes the actions to be carried out by each of the agents who will intervene in the building. More than the design of some choral action in which all the individual efforts will be integrated in the architectonic object, the project resembles a film script—the document that must preestablish the field of action for the multiple technical agents deployed. At the limit, the project must figure all of the determinants of the final object: not only its formal description, but also the logistics of its mise-en-scène.

In the ninth section of "The Work of Art," Benjamin writes that the nature of the cinematographic illusion is of the second order, because in it there is neither a definite emplacement nor a place in which the filming of each scene has taken place in any genuine fashion. For the work of modern architecture, the place and the modes of action of each technique must be feigned in the project in such a way that the real production need not depend on either the circumstances of the temporal moment or the decisions demanded by the place at the time of intervention. The architectonic modus operandi must be delineated entirely within the fictitious scenario of the project in such a way that the agents who are to intervene in its production can follow the script determined in advance by the project itself. Because place must be technically, abstractly, and disjunctively controlled in the program of actions determined by the project, it is only retrospectively that we can imagine an architecture determined by the benevolent action of some immeasurable genius loci.

In the project of montage and assembly, the architect is not personally responsible for any of the multiple aspects that come together in the material production of the architectonic object. Just as the film director is not personally responsible for the script, wardrobe, sets, or shots of each sequence, neither does the architect have some specially privileged role in the siting, volume, structure, envelope, or cladding of a project: each forms part of the technical diffraction of the architectonic object; none can nor should play a principal or decisive role. Only the montage, the skilled, painstaking, and conflictive bringing together of all of the elements, is decisive. A bringing together that can never be a *Gesamtkunstwerk*, the felicitous uniting of all the arts and all the crafts, without the laborious articulation of drawings, spatial decisions, choice of components, etc.

That everything is decided in the montage does not mean that the work—cinematographic or architectonic— must be anonymous, banal, or without signification. On the contrary: the importance Benjamin accords the montage stems from his enthusiastic response to Russian cinema. Just as Sergei Eisenstein's framing, lighting, black and white toning, and musical choice are no more than component parts of a work whose montage embodies all of the crucial decisions of the script, so too in contemporary architecture the decisive moment consists of the skill and intelligence with which the architect puts together the contributions of all the operators of the building in the space and time of the project. A project is, by definition, a technical instrument that allows for the reproduction of the work of architecture after it has first been assembled in the virtual and fictitious space of the design: a set of protocols drawn up in professional offices that many people, by no means accidentally, call studios.

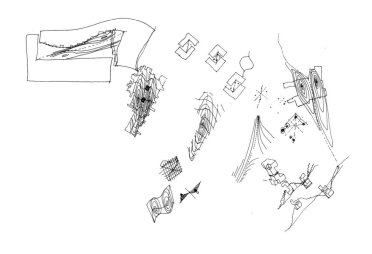

The genre known as architectural criticism does not occupy the Olympian heights or consolidated position the term might seem to suggest. Criticism—from the Indo-European root *Krhtes*—is judgment. But we have been aware for quite some time now that judging and dispensing justice is not so much a sovereign act of pure reason as a practice that guides social behavior by means of mechanisms that are the products of convention, power, and the fortuitous encounter between judge and defendant. At the present time, criticism closely resembles hand-to-hand combat: a contest between information seeking public recognition and the power of collective sanction vested in those supposedly able to bestow it. In a changing society that questions its own foundations, and in a culture that must compose anew each day its very structures of thought, what corresponds to critical confrontation is any kind of encounter marked by violence.

In modern culture, those who engage in architectural criticism are unable easily to carry

ten **Sado-masochism: Criticism and Architectural Practice**

out that distancing of anxiety which Manfredo Tàfuri so lucidly invokes in the first sentence of his book *Teorie e storie dell'architettura*. There is no one historical, technical, or visual knowledge. The scientific history of positivism has given way to narration; the articulation of material conditions that structured the need for facts has been replaced by microhistory, the universes of mentalities, and the emergence of a new subjectivism.

It is impossible today to write a treatise on architecture, since it is impossible to order, hierarchically and homogeneously, the sum of changing technical data and knowledge, constantly added to, deploying itself according to strategies that no longer have anything to do with the protective support of science, particularly when science is engaged in looking for its own foundations in unpredictability and catastrophe. There is not one vision, but many. The images that surround us and bombard our sensibilities are fragments of diverse systems; and the construction of visual memory is completely different in a rural environment than in an urban one, different for a taxi driver and a painter, for a photographer and an aircraft pilot.

In this situation, criticism spreads out and deploys itself, looking for reasons in what Deleuze has called folds of knowledge, provisional coagulations of truth upon which to set the scales of justice. In his distancing of the object and in the unsteadiness of his arguments, the critic controls his own anxiety by means of a compensatory aggressiveness. The sadism latent in contemporary criticism is not a private perversity of those who exercise it but a *mal du siècle*, the evident manifestation of a syndrome that affects relations with the universe of facts and thus also with the world of architectural objects. But the sadism of the critics symmetrically corresponds to the masochism of the practicing architects. Patient producers of artifacts whose meaning does not reveal itself naturally or evidently, the architects approach with their works on their backs, resigned to receive the lashes of their chastisers.

Oh, that there were a discipline of architecture! If there were only a knowledge, not craft-based and empirical but general and logically transferrable, then the insecurities of those working on the practical side would be deliciously alleviated. There was a time when the knowledge needed to produce architecture could be encapsulated in the lessons derived from experience of the trade. The general, cultural, and social framework of this practice was never called into question; it was solidly established. Architecture was, in these times, an exquisite material labor capable of producing beautiful results; it was not a global discourse addressing the great questions filling individual consciences with uncertainty. Architecture instead resembled the beautiful work of the potter who forms vessels with his or her dextrous hands, constituting the proof of a perfect fit between the conditions of the material and a wisdom that is implicit.

In recent years there has been an outpouring of anxious calls to return to the craft. These outcries manifest a desire to discover in the dexterity of the architect's eye and hand the ability to distance the anxiety of a formative activity that had suddenly found itself dumb and blind. From the moment when the ideological system constructed by the historic avant-gardes collapsed and the modern project turned problematic, it was no longer possible to design everything from a chair to a city with the same assurance possessed by the architects of the generation of the great masters.

Given that practice itself lacks a discourse, architecture reluctantly finds itself in need of some means for understanding what lies beyond the concrete framework of a particular building. Almost without exception, contemporary architectural journals reveal, in their awkward dissociation between text and image, the real dissociation between object and discourse, between practice and criticism. The perversely masochistic resignation with which the architect invites the critic to speak reveals with absolute clarity the pathology of a relationship based more on distancing and fear than on some paradisal dialogue, harmoniously animated by the light of truth.

Is it possible to develop an internal critique, a discourse articulated out of reach of the great debates and crises of contemporary thought? Such a possibility constitutes perhaps an illusion, a vain hope, but at the same time a necessity. Judgments cannot be removed from the more general parameters of cultural debate. To imagine that a space could be set aside along the fringes of contemporary thought for the analysis, problematization, and internal articulation of the discipline is pure fantasy—a defensive posture that seeks to exclude architecture and architects from the cultural universe. Those who cry out in vexation, "Let us speak alone amongst ourselves, of our own affairs!" reveal not only their absolute want of courage but also their allegiance to the legion of those whom Nietzsche called the children of resignation.

There is nevertheless a critical attitude that is perfectly possible but is at the present moment blocked by the sadism of some and the masochism of others. It is possible to construct an internal discourse based on experience and actual practice but avoiding the purely autobiographical. The contemporary discourse by architects on architecture has not yet reached that level of critical judgment, that holistic cultural confrontation. It is a necessary voice, as indispensable as that of any other cultural agent seeking to intervene in the construction of meaning. To understand one's own work, to be able to problematize it, calls for a certain estrangement, an operation of alienation in the strictest etymological sense of the term.

The works of Viollet-le-Duc, Gottfried Semper, and Otto Wagner provide suggestive examples of the discourse of architects on architecture. They never, fortunately, presumed to constitute treatises; their work is of value not for its perfection of a system but because it represents the explicit reflection of an experience. Faced with the crisis of the encyclopedias, these architects, whose commitment was to practice above all, were nevertheless capable of articulating a discourse. Experience, history, and project are interwoven throughout their writings, which reveal nothing other than the verbal articulation—transmissible and logical—of a practice. It is not criticism; it is not history; it is not a treatise; nor should it be. But it is an endeavor to escape the isolation of the professional studio, the closed domain of works, projects, and pure experience, in the hopes of finding a word worthy of being heard.

Bibliography

one **Topographies of Contemporary Architecture**

De Zurko, Edward R. *Origins of Functionalist Theory*. New York: Columbia University Press, 1957.

Giedion, Sigfried. *Space, Time and Architecture: The Growth of a New Tradition*. Cambridge: Harvard University Press, 1941.

Jung, Carl Gustav. *Psychologische Typen*. Zurich: Rascher, 1921.

Merleau-Ponty, Maurice. *Phenomenologie de la perception*. Paris: Gallimard, 1945.

Merleau-Ponty, Maurice. "Le primat de la perception et des conséquences philosophiques." *Bulletin de la Société Française de Philosophie* 41, no. 4 (October-December 1947).

Pevsner, Nikolaus. "The Picturesque in Architecture." *Journal of the Royal Institute of British Architects* 55 (December 1947).

two **Mies van der Rohe and Minimalism**

Barthes, Roland. *Le degré zéro de l'écriture*. Paris: Éditions du Seuil, 1953. Translated as *Writing Degree Zero*, trans. Annette Lavers and Colin Smith. New York: Hill and Wang, 1968.

Benjamin, Walter. "Kleine Geschichte der Photographie," 1931. In *Gesammelte Schriften*, 2(1): 368–385. Frankfurt: Suhrkamp, 1974–1982. Translated as "A Small History of Photography," trans. Edmund Jephcott and Kingsley Shorter. In *One-Way Street and Other Writings*, 240–257. London: NLB, 1979.

De Duve, Thierry. *Nominalisme pictural*. Paris: Éditions de Minuit, 1984. Translated as *Pictorial Nominalism: On Marcel Duchamp's Passage from Painting to the Readymade*, trans. Dana Polan and the author. Minneapolis: University of Minnesota Press, 1991.

Deleuze, Gilles. *Différence et répétition*. Paris: Presses Universitaires de France, 1968. Translated as *Difference and Repetition*, trans. Paul Patton. New York: Columbia University Press, 1994.

Deleuze, Gilles, and Félix Guattari. *Qu'est-ce que la philosophie?* Paris: Éditions de Minuit, 1991. Translated as *What Is Philosophy?*, trans. Hugh Tomlinson and Graham Burchell. New York: Columbia University Press, 1994.

Neumeyer, Fritz. *Mies van der Rohe. Das kunstlose Wort. Gedanken zur Baukunst*. Berlin: Wolf Jobst Siedler, 1986. Translated as *The Artless Word*, trans. Mark Jarzombek. Cambridge: MIT Press, 1991.

three **Architecture and Existentialism**

Heidegger, Martin. *Über den Humanismus*. Frankfurt am Main: Klostermann, 1947.

Merleau-Ponty, Maurice. *Humanisme et terreur*. Paris: Gallimard, 1947.

Tyrwhitt, J., J. L. Sert, and E. N. Rogers. *The Heart of the City: Towards the Humanisation of Urban Life*. London: CIAM VIII, 1952.

four **Weak Architecture**

Deleuze, Gilles. *Foucault*. Paris: Éditions de Minuit, 1986.

Heidegger, Martin. *Die Kunst und der Raum*. St. Gallen: Erker Verlag, 1969.

Tafuri, Manfredo. "Realismus und Architektur: zur Konstruktion volksbezogner Sprachen." In Vittorio Magnago Lampugnani, ed., *Das Abenteurer der Ideen*, 131–147. Berlin: Internationale Bauausstellung, 1994. First published as "Réalisme et architecture," *Critique* 476–477 (January-February 1987).

Trias, Eugenio. *Los límites del mundo*. Barcelona: Ariel, 1985.

Vattimo, Gianni. *La fine della modernità*. Milan: Garzanti, 1985.

five **From Autonomy to Untimeliness**

Deleuze, Gilles, and Félix Guattari. *Mille plateaux*. Paris: Éditions de Minuit, 1980.

Gadamer, Hans-Georg. *Wahrheit und Methode*. Tübingen: J. C. B. Mohr Verlag, 1960.

Jauss, Hans Robert. *Aesthetische Erfahrung und literarische Hermeneutik*. Munich: W. Fink Verlag, 1977.

Judd, Donald. *Architektur*. Münster: Westfälischer Kunstverein, 1989.

six **Place: Permanence or Production**

Deleuze, Gilles. *Pourparleurs 1972–1990*. Paris: Éditions de Minuit, 1990.

Detienne, Marcel, ed. *Traces de fondation*. Paris: Peeters, Lourain, 1990.

Lyotard, Jean-François. *Leçons sur l'analytique du sublime*. Paris: Galilée, 1991.

Norberg-Schulz, Christian. *Genius Loci*. New York: Rizzoli, 1980.

Rykwert, Joseph. *The Idea of a Town: The Anthropology of Urban Form in Rome, Italy and the Ancient World*. Princeton, N.J.: Princeton University Press, 1976.

seven   **Difference and Limit: Individualism in Contemporary Architecture**
Deleuze, Gilles. *Différence et répétition*. Paris: Presses Universitaires de France, 1968.

Derrida, Jacques. *L'écriture et la différence*. Paris: Le Seuil, 1967.

Trías, Eugenio. *Lógica del límite*. Barcelona: Destino, 1991.

eight   **High Tech: Functionalism or Rhetoric**
Heidegger, Martin. *Die Technik und die Kehre*. Pfullingen: Neske, 1962.

Jünger, Ernst. *Der Arbeiter*. Hamburg: Hanseatische Verlagsanstalt, 1932.

Le Corbusier. *Vers une architecture*. Paris: G. Crès, 1923.

Tafuri, Manfredo. *Progetto e utopia*. Bari: Laterza, 1973. Translated as *Architecture and Utopia: Design and Capitalist Development*, trans. Barbara Luigia La Penta (Cambridge: MIT Press, 1976).

nine   **The Work of Architecture in the Age of Mechanical Reproduction**
Benjamin, Walter. "Das Kunstwerk in Zeitalter seiner technischen Reproduzierbarkeit." In *Schriften*. Frankfurt am Main: Suhrkamp Verlag, 1955. Translated as "The Work of Art in the Age of Mechanical Reproduction." In *Illuminations*, ed. Hannah Arendt, trans. Harry Zohn. New York: Schocken Books, 1969.

ten   **Sado-masochism: Criticism and Architectural Practice**
Ginzburg, Carlo, and Adriano Prosperi. *Giochi di pazienza*. Turin: Giulio Einaudi, 1975.

Tafuri, Manfredo. *La sfera e il laberinto*. Turin: Giulio Einaudi, 1980. Translated as *The Sphere and the Labyrinth*, trans. Pellegrino d'Acierno and Robert Connolly. Cambridge: MIT Press, 1987.

Warning, Rainer, ed. *Rezeptionsaesthetik: Teoria und Praxis*. Munich: Wilhom Fink Verlag, 1979.

Note on Sources

With certain modifications, most of the texts included here appeared between 1987 and 1993 in various books and publications. The selection, ordering, and structure of these texts constitute a line of argumentation with which I have sought to express my view of the situation of architecture at the end of the twentieth century.

Chapter 2, "Mies van der Rohe and Minimalism," appeared in *The Presence of Mies*, edited by Detlef Mertins (New York: Princeton Architectural Press, 1994).

Chapter 3, "Architecture and Existentialism," appeared as "Architettura e esistenzialismo: una crisi dell'architettura moderna," *Casabella* no. 583 (Milan, October 1991).

Chapter 4, "Weak Architecture," appeared as "Arquitectura Dédil/Weak Architecture," *Quaderns d'Arquitectura i Urbanisme* no. 175 (Barcelona, October-December 1987).

Chapter 5, "From Autonomy to Untimeliness," appeared in *Anyone*, edited by Cynthia C. Davidson (New York: Rizzoli, December 1991).

Chapter 6, "Place: Permanence or Production," appeared in *Anywhere*, edited by Cynthia C. Davidson (New York: Rizzoli, 1992).

Chapter 7, "Difference and Limit: Individualism in Contemporary Architecture," appeared as "Differenza e limite: individualismo nell'architettura contemporanea," *Domus* no. 736 (Milan, March 1992).

Chapter 8, "High Tech: Functionalism or Rhetoric," appeared in *Functionalism: Utopia or the Way Forward*, The 5th International Alvar Aalto Symposium, August 16–18, 1991 (Jyväskylä: Alvar Aalto Symposium, 1992).

Chapter 9, "The Work of Art in the Age of Mechanical Reproduction," appeared as "Un approccio benjaminiano al progetto architettonico," *Lotus International* no. 71 (Milan, 2nd quarter 1992).

Chapter 10, "Sado-masochism: Criticism and Architectural Practice," appeared as "Sadomasochismo, overo, la critica e la pratica architettonica," *Casabella* no. 545 (Milan, April 1988).

Illustration Credits

Introduction: Frank O. Gehry, Villa Olímpica, Barcelona, 1990

Chapter 1: Juan Navarro Baldeweg, Salamanca Conference and Exhibition Hall and Conference Center, Salamanca, 1985

Chapter 2: Mies van der Rohe, Concert Hall, 1944

Chapter 3: Arata Isozaki, Sant Jordi Palace, Barcelona, 1983

Chapter 4: Alvaro Siza, Faculty of Architecture, Oporto, 1988

Chapter 5: Frank O. Gehry, Walt Disney Auditorium, Los Angeles, 1989

Chapter 6: Tadao Ando, Time's II Project, Nakagyo, Kyoto, 1986

Chapter 7: Jacques Herzog and Pierre de Meuron, Ricola Building, Laufen, 1986

Chapter 8: Norman Foster, Hong Kong & Shanghai Banking Corporation, Hong Kong, 1979

Chapter 9: Rem Koolhaas, Congrexpo Project, Lille, 1992

Chapter 10: Peter Eisenman, Submission to the International Seminar of Design for Cannaregio, Venice: Diagrams showing topological deformation of site plan horizontally and vertically, 1978. Collection Centre Canadien d'Architecture/Canadian Centre for Architecture

Index of Names